Connie Mack's
BASEBALL BOOK

Connie Mack's BASEBALL BOOK

FOREWORD BY RED SMITH

Illustrated by Floyd Torbert

NEW YORK: ALFRED A. KNOPF

1950

THIS IS A BORZOI BOOK,
PUBLISHED BY ALFRED A. KNOPF, INC.

Copyright 1950 by Connie Mack. All rights reserved. No part of this book may be reproduced in any form without permission in writing from the publisher, except by a reviewer who may quote brief passages and reproduce not more than three illustrations in a review to be printed in a magazine or newspaper. Manufactured in the United States of America. Published simultaneously in Canada by McClelland & Stewart Limited.

Published April 17, 1950
First & Second Printing Before Publication

FOREWORD

A CLEVELAND outfielder named Oris Hockett, cut off trying to score, was chased back to third base by the Athletics' catcher. There he found the bag occupied by Lou Boudreau, who had advanced from second on the play. Hockett shrugged, relinquishing the base to his manager, and jogged on out the left field line. The Philadelphia catcher touched Boudreau with the ball, then pursued and tagged Hockett. The A's made a perfunctory argument for a double play.

"Nonsense," the umpires said. "Boudreau was tagged standing safely on the bag. Only Hockett is out." Everybody in Cleveland's Municipal Stadium concurred. Everybody, that is, save Connie Mack, who thrust his gray head out of the dugout and beckoned.

Joe Rue came scampering in response to the summons. I forget who the other umpires were but Willie Grieve was not one of them.

"Don't you think, Mr. Grieve," said the Philadelphia manager, "that the play went this way? When Hockett ran back past third, that put Boudreau ahead of him. So Boudreau is out for passing a preceding runner. Hockett, of course, was tagged in left field, so he's out. Double play."

"Keerect," said Mr. Rue, "and thank you, sir."

I know no other story so characteristic of Connie Mack, the only man in the ball park who could, in the same breath, call the play right and the umpire's name wrong. Ever since the days of Addie Joss (whom he called "Josh") Connie Mack has been slow on names and one jump ahead of everyone else on baseball.

One jump? Well, listen: later in that same game, the Athletics' Bobby Estalella hit a ground ball and reached first base on an infielder's wild throw. He ran across the bag, turned around to his left and was ambling back when the first baseman, recovering a rebound from the grandstand wall, tagged him. The rookie umpire working at first base called Estalella out.

Now, years ago the rules provided that a batsman overrunning first base was entitled to return safely on condition that he make the turn to his right, away from second. Later the rule was changed to allow him to turn either way, provided he made no attempt to go on to second base. It was obvious that the young umpire, rattled, had applied the old rule.

His decision stuck. After the game, which Philadelphia lost, the umpires stopped by to thank Mr. Mack again for helping them out on the play at third.

"That's all right," Connie said, and he turned a

[FOREWORD]

guileless smile on the rookie umpire. "Ah, on that play at first, Estalella turned the wrong way, didn't he?"

"No," said the young man, who'd had several innings to repent his error and get his story straight, "I thought he made a break for second." So he avoided the trap which Connie, two jumps ahead of everyone, was laying for him.

Two jumps? Let's count again. Talking over the game that night, Connie said: "We were leading when that play happened at third. If I'd a knowed we were going to lose, I'd have let them call it wrong. Then I could have protested the game and it would have had to be replayed."

See where he was all the time? Three jumps ahead.

In January of 1940 there was a banquet in Philadelphia. The Yankees had won four consecutive pennants, four consecutive world championships. They were matchless, unconquerable. The Athletics had spent six years in the second division, three of them in last place. Connie Mack arose to address the diners.

"I am going to stick my neck out," he said, "and make two predictions. The Athletics will defeat the Yankees on opening day. The Yankees will finish third this year."

Two and a half months later, the Athletics opened the season by beating the Yankees. Eight months after Connie's forecast, the Yankees finished third.

Connie sat chatting in the dugout one afternoon before a game in Detroit. "We'll win this one," he said. "Gehringer's going to have a bad day."

This was in the era when Charley Gehringer was without a peer at second base. He simply never had a bad day. That afternoon he made several errors on crucial plays, and the Athletics won.

"I don't know," Connie said when asked how psychic a guy could get. "I was watching Charley at infield practice. He didn't seem to have that rhythm, somehow."

There was one winter when it was practically a hanging offense to publish a national magazine without a picture of Lou Novikoff on the cover. The young man was coming up to the Cubs, leaving a minor league trail dotted with the bleached bones of pitchers. That spring both the Cubs and Athletics trained on the Pacific Coast.

"There'll be a lot of question about that young man," Connie said after seeing Novikoff in one exhibition game. "I think he can be pitched to."

Novikoff came East with the Cubs, and National League pitchers chased him back to the bushes.

That may have been the spring when Connie postponed for weeks the task of telling a rookie that he'd have to return to the minors for more schooling. On the last day in camp, Connie was miserable. He'd have to break the news that day.

"After all my years," he confessed, "there are two things I've never got used to: haggling with a player over his contract, and telling a boy he's got to go back."

I've been trying to sketch a picture of the man whose book this is, but it is a hopeless job. As a newspaperman covering the Athletics, I traveled with him for ten years, from Philadelphia to Mexico City, from San Diego to Boston. It would take me ten years to tell about him— a towering figure, with the humility of the truly great.

"I was never a good manager of a bad ball club, prob-

[FOREWORD]

ably the worst," he said one time. And again: "I have never known a day when I didn't learn something new about this game."

He has been studying his lessons daily for sixty-eight years. Now he gives the result to the reader.

RED SMITH

CONTENTS

THE GAME	3
GETTING YOUR CHANCE	12
THE SCOUT LOOKS YOU OVER	24
WHAT I LOOK FOR IN A ROOKIE	36
WHICH POSITION DO YOU WANT TO PLAY?	54
THE BATTER	66
PITCHING	81

[CONTENTS]

THE CATCHER	98
FIRST AND THIRD BASE	112
SECOND BASE AND SHORTSTOP	123
THE OUTFIELD	132
BASE RUNNING	144
TEAM PLAY	156
COACHING, TEAM SIGNALS AND SCORING	169
THE CONTRACT	184
WHAT CAN YOU GET OUT OF BASEBALL?	195
Let's Look at the Records	205
Glossary of Baseball Terms	227
Index *follows page*	234

Connie Mack's
BASEBALL BOOK

The Athletics' shortstop Eddie Joost in action.

Joe tried hard, but the throw beat him home.

Al Gionfriddo stops Joe DiMaggio's blast and saves a World Series game for the Dodgers.

ACME PHOTO

Phil Rizzuto, Yankee shortstop, takes to the air as Jackie Robinson slides into second.

Pee Wee Reese gains altitude to nab the throw, but too late to catch Bill Rigney (Giants), stealing second base.

ACME PHOT

Joe DiMaggio hook-slides safely into second base.

Stan Musial wallops one to right field.

ACME PHOTO

Carl Furillo is safe at first as Ed Waitkus (Phillies) stretches for the ball.

Stan Hack (Cubs), caught between first and second, is tagged out by second baseman Eddie Mayo (3). Rudy York, first baseman, blocks Hack's path to the base.

ACME PHOTO

Joe smashes out a home run.

The late Lou Gehrig singles, in his 2000th consecutive game.

ACME PHOTO

ACME PHOTO

An attempted bunt by Al Schoendienst (Cardinals) goes foul as Bruce Edwards (Dodgers) and umpire follow the ball.

A sacrifice bunt by Howie Pollet (Cardinals) that failed.

ACME PHO

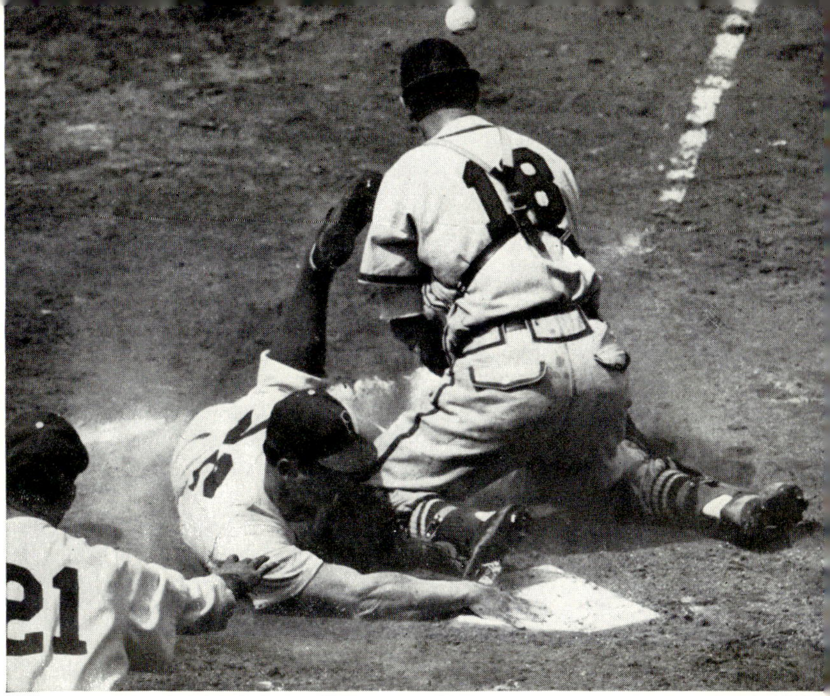

ACME PHOTO

Gene Hermanski (Dodgers) reaches for the plate as Del Rice (Cardinals) blocks him, but can't handle the throw-in.

Steve Gromek (Indians) hurtles through the air after piling into Bob Swift (Tigers) to score a deciding run.

ACME PHOTO

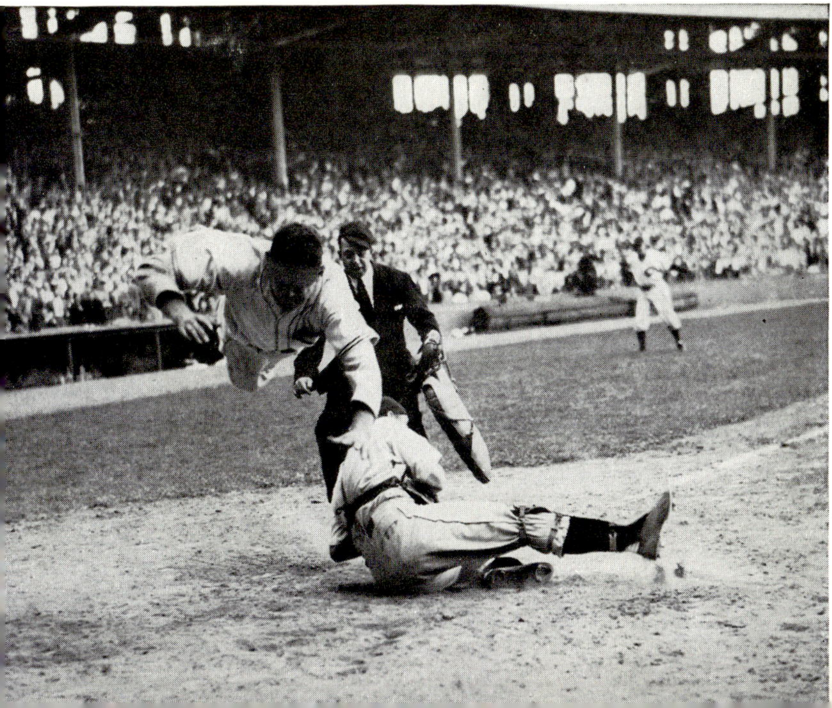

ACME PHOTO

Birdie Tebbets (Tigers) plants his foot out to keep Ted Williams from scoring.

Stan Musial safe after smacking a homer. Mickey Owen (Cubs) attempts the putout, as pitcher Bob Chipman backs him up.

ACME PHOTO

Pitcher Lou Brissie

Connie Mack greets his men at West Palm Beach Training Camp

THE GAME

Long before the dawn of written history, games had been devised in which small round objects were used in various ways. They were used in games for pleasure by the common people; sometimes they were used by the priests in religious ceremonies.

Homer, the ancient Greek poet, writes of a form of handball that was played by the Greeks. In Egypt, the priests of the god Osiris threw a ball around in the rites sacred to their worship. Across the ocean in a world as yet undiscovered by the white man, in the peninsula of Yucatan, the Mayas played a game with a ball and the playing field was a part of the precinct of the gods of the temple.

The pastimes of people during the Dark Ages have been largely lost to view, but as the light of reason reappears in history, ball games also begin to reappear, particularly in England. First came handball, in which only the ball and the hand were employed.

Later, from France, was imported tennis, in which the racquet, or bat, appears for the first time. From handball and tennis there developed a number of pastimes all more or less based on the same principles.

None of these, however, was baseball.

Baseball is completely American in its origin and its development. Until recently it was the Great *American* Game. It is now also the Great Japanese Game, for the Japanese are hotter, madder baseball fans than the wild-eyed rooters of any great American city.

Go anywhere in Central America—Cuba, Mexico, Venezuela, Puerto Rico—and there, too, you will find the populace baseball crazy. The Latin-Americans have invented a new word to describe the game: "*Beisbol*," as well as many other new Spanish words used in the language of the game.

Indeed, Mexico has its organized league, and a few years ago some mighty good American players were lured south of the border to play in that league. In Cuba, it is said, a boy gets a baseball glove as soon as he is able to walk, and there are no greater heroes to the Cubans than their baseball stars.

During World War II baseball was popularized around the world by the U. S. armed forces. Wherever they went, from the coral rocks in mid-Pacific to the icy reaches of frozen Greenland, they took the pastime with them. Not only that; you could almost always find a major or minor league star at an Army or Navy installation around whom a team could be formed.

[THE GAME]

So the game of baseball was given worldwide demonstration in this way. It didn't take everywhere. Europe still holds aloof from it, but it is now well established as a popular pastime in South America.

Take Quito, in Ecuador, for instance. It is located at an altitude of 9500 feet above sea level in the Andes. You can't throw a curve at that altitude; the air is too thin. But curves or no curves, there are several baseball teams there, and the University of Quito has made baseball a part of its sports program. Incidentally, the Quito players tested all kinds of native wood for use in making bats and decided that eucalyptus wood was best.

The Pan-American countries hold their own World Series with the champion team in each nation's league meeting in the playoffs; finally the winners battle it out in the Latin-American World Series.

So you see, millions of men and boys play baseball not only in the U. S. A. but in many other countries, too. Countless men and women and boys and girls watch the game as it is played in major- and minor-league ball parks, on semi-pro diamonds, on high school and college baseball fields and finally, on the sand lots and grassy stretches of a million recreation parks and playgrounds everywhere in this big country of ours.

That's why it is so hard to answer the question: "Where do they come from?" that I am so often asked about big league ball players.

They come from everywhere. The reason: Because baseball is so American. There is not a hamlet or village where you will not find a baseball diamond and a makeshift team of sorts. There is not a spot anywhere in the three million square miles of America to which the radio does not penetrate to carry the game play by play, or that failing, to give the daily scores and perhaps a little gossip of the diamond.

Television, too, is bringing the game into the living rooms of millions of American homes, adding to the popularity of the pastime.

To me it is not strange that the majority of the players on the major league teams come from small towns, places that most of us would never get to hear about if some great baseball star didn't make his way from the local semi-pro team into the minors and then achieve the big jump to the majors.

Next time you go to a baseball game get a program and read the roster of players. In addition to the weight, height and batting average of the players you will find beside each one's name the name of his home town. Read that list carefully. It should convince you of two things: First, that baseball is played in other places besides the cities with big league teams, and second, that you don't have to come from a big town to make the grade. A small town player, if he has the requirements, can make it just as well.

Have you ever heard of a town called Factoryville? Probably not. It's not a very consequential place. It is located in northeast Pennsylvania, about twenty miles from the city of Scranton. I mention it as a case in point, because it was from Factoryville that one of the greatest pitchers in baseball history came. His name was Christy Mathewson, and because his rise to fame in the major leagues from a small-town beginning should be an inspi-

[THE GAME]

ration to every boy who hopes to do likewise, I am going to tell his story here.

Matty liked to play baseball from the first. He was quite big for his age and his schoolmates called him "Husk." He fancied himself a pitcher but to qualify for the Factoryville semi-pro team as a moundsman he had to strike out every one on the team. One afternoon he did just that very thing, on the main street of the town, while virtually every resident of Factoryville watched in amazement.

He then enrolled at nearby Keystone Academy, where he ultimately became captain of the team. Matty's baseball idol was John McGraw, then manager of the Baltimore Orioles and later to become his manager with the New York Giants. In after years, Matty and his wife lived with the McGraws.

Matty followed McGraw's strategy in his own schoolboy baseball. He would not pitch except against a very strong rival team but stationed himself at second base. When the psychological moment came, he would take over the pitching, and he was so skilful with his curves and fast ball that before long he was hailed as the best scholastic pitcher in Pennsylvania.

At the end of the Academy term, he pitched a few games for a semi-professional team. His pay was a dollar per game. Then the Honesdale, Pennsylvania, team offered him twenty dollars a month if he would sign up as a pitcher. He took the job and as fate would have it, here he met the former big-league player who taught him the curve that was to become world-famous as the "fadeaway."

Matty knew a good pitch when he saw one. He practiced the fadeaway for hours on end until he had virtually perfect control. He used the pitch very seldom, however, preferring to keep it under wraps until he needed to fall back upon it.

After the Academy, Matty matriculated at Bucknell University and made not only the baseball nine but the football team, too. He was as phenomenal on the gridiron as he was on the diamond. While at college, he signed to play with the Norfolk, Virginia, team upon his graduation.

From Norfolk his fame spread. The Norfolk team sold him to three different clubs at the same time, the Athletics included. We took the matter to court, but the Giants won out and Matty went to New York to play. In subsequent World Series I had cause for great regret that Matty wasn't on my side.

When he first reported for training, George Davis, then manager of the Giants, asked him: "What have you got on the ball?"

Matty showed him his regular assortment, and Davis asked: "Anything else?" Whereupon Matty let loose his "fadeaway." Davis couldn't touch it. He instructed Matty to concentrate on the delivery and when the newspaper writers got wind of it, Matty was given great publicity as the master of a new method of pitching.

Christy Mathewson was not only a great baseball player but he was a fine man, too. By his living example he helped to raise the game of baseball in the eyes of many who did not up to that time have a high opinion of

[THE GAME]

the game. He took his profession very seriously and was devoted to it.

Matty had wonderful control of the ball, but in those days, when a good many pitchers used the "bean" ball in an effort to intimidate the batter, he would never do so.

I remember distinctly how Frank Baker, the Athletics' third baseman in the World Series against the Giants in 1911, earned his nickname of "Home Run" Baker. In the last inning of the third game, Matty had two strikes on Baker. Waiting out a couple of pitches, Baker hit the ball into the rightfield stand. That home run ended the game in a victory for the Athletics and won for Frank Baker a sobriquet which he still wears.

I asked Baker later why he took a chance waiting for the right pitch. "I knew Matty wouldn't hit me," he said. "So I just waited for a good one."

Yes, Matty was a small-town boy who made extra good in the big leagues. There are many more who do it every year.

Some come from far away places like Puerto Rico and from the South American countries. I believe I was the first manager to sign a South American to a major league contract. He was Jud Castro, a second baseman on the Athletics' team in 1902, and hailed from Venezuela. He had been a student at Holy Cross and showed some promise of being a top-notch baseball player so I signed him up.

Later, of course, many more Latin-Americans came into the big leagues. Clark Griffith, who was then manager of the Cincinnati Reds, introduced quite a few of the

Spanish-speaking "*beisboleros*" into the major leagues around 1910.

There is a story told about a player named Rafael Almeida who had made quite a name for himself in the Cuban League, when Griffith sent for him to come to Cincinnati for a try-out.

Almeida didn't speak a word of English so he brought along with him an interpreter named Armando Marsans. When the time came for Almeida's tryout, Marsans went on the field to help Almeida warm up.

Griffith took one look at the pair warming up and said: "I like his interpreter better," and signed up Marsans.

I have two Cubans on my Athletics team at present. One is Roberto Estalella, a utility outfielder, and the other is my first-string catcher, Fermin (Mike) Guerra. In the spring and summer, Mike plays with the Athletics; in the winter, when it is warm and balmy in Cuba, he is the manager of the Almendares (Cuban League) team. Mike loves the game so well he manages to play it all year round.

Among the other Latin-Americans who have made great names for themselves in major-league baseball are Adolfo Luque, famed Giants' pitcher, and Miguel (Mike) Gonzales, well-remembered Cardinals' catcher, and presently two of the ablest coaches in the business.

Stories about these two are legion. Gonzales once stole home in a game in which Grover Alexander was pitching against the Cardinals. Miller Huggins, who was then manager of the Cardinals, said to Gonzales as the latter sidled toward him on the bench: "You stole home without my signal. You've got plenty of nerve."

[THE GAME]

"I also got plenty of lead," chortled Gonzales.

On another occasion, Gonzales, who later became a scout for the Giants, was sent by Manager McGraw to look over a minor-league prospect. Completing his assignment, he sent McGraw a telegram which has since become a classic in baseball: "Good field, no hit. Mike." The prospect was not signed up.

But no matter where they come from, in my opinion the big thing about baseball is that if a fellow has the ability there's no limit to the heights to which he can rise.

Is anyone who loves baseball ever going to forget little Pepper Martin of the St. Louis Cardinals in the World Series of 1931? In the second game of that series he made two hits, stole two bases and scored the only two runs of the game. He had the Athletics so rattled with his daring base-stealing that he even made Mickey Cochrane overthrow second base, and Mickey didn't do that very often.

Yet Pepper Martin had to "hop" a ride on a freight train to get to his major league tryout.

What about Dizzy Dean? He rode to the heights on a great pitching arm and his unbelievable self-confidence. Yet where did he start? As a ragged cotton picker on a Southern farm. Who will ever forget the season when Dizzy and his brother Paul pitched the Cardinals to a pennant with forty-nine games won between them?

There are hundreds and hundreds of similar instances of young fellows who started their baseball careers on the lowest rungs of the ladder. But inevitably their ability, their sportsmanship and their quality became known, and anyone who has the combination of these three will not, *cannot* be kept down.

GETTING YOUR CHANCE

IF, as I have said before, there are only 400 players comprising the sixteen major league teams, and if there are four million young Americans playing the game in any one year, you may ask: "How do I get a chance to play in the big leagues?"

This is a very fair question and to answer it I am going to have to give you an account of how baseball is organized. First, however, I want to say emphatically that if you are ever to play in the big leagues, you must start at the bottom of organized baseball.

Now the term "organized baseball" doesn't necessarily mean the professional leagues. It does mean an aggregation of teams, however, that play with fair regularity, that play under rules, and whose members receive some degree of instruction. These can be a Junior High School league, or a church denominational league, or any one

[GETTING YOUR CHANCE]

of the many leagues for young fellows that have been organized throughout the country by the American Legion and from whose ranks have come so many splendid big league players.

There is a definite advantage in playing in an organized league. For one thing it gives you an opportunity to play repeat games against a team in competition with which you may have fared not too well the first time. It also develops team spirit, which is enormously important in major-league play, and for the first time it teaches you to play with a group rather than merely as an individual.

Besides all this, you are quite certain to meet youngsters who know something more about the game and how it should be played than you may know and from whom you can gain a great deal of practical knowledge about baseball. You can also establish friendships with boys of your own age who have the same love of the game as yourself.

Another advantage of belonging to an organized baseball group is that you will tend under such an organization to fit yourself better physically for the game. If you play baseball individually only when the spirit moves you, you are not apt to go out for practice except for a short while before a game is to be played. But if you are a member of a team that plays regularly the chances are that the coach or the captain is going to see to it that you get plenty of practice and instruction between games and at the specified times when the other members of the team will practice with you. Thus your co-ordination and team play will be developed.

Now let's suppose that you have gone through junior high school and are in your closing years at high school or perhaps even in college. You have what you consider the makings of a fine baseball player. Your coach agrees with you, and you have made up your mind that you would like to become a professional baseball player. What's the next step? Well, it may be that baseball already has its eye on you. Every year up and down the length of this country and into Canada, Cuba and Mexico, there travel professional baseball scouts. Very often without knowing it, the young fellows involved are watched carefully in play. The Athletics alone employ twenty professional scouts who are all former big league stars now retired from the active game or who have served a period as coaches and who know the requirements for a big league player.

Every day of the year I receive by either mail, telegraph or telephone advice from someone, either a former player or a team manager or even a fan who has appointed himself a semiofficial scout for the Athletics, telling me that somewhere in the hinterland there is a young fellow who will be a second Christy Mathewson on the mound or another Lou Gehrig at the bat.

We investigate all these tips, and where the circumstances warrant, a scout is sent to watch the particular player in action. If his play measures up to the scout's standard, and if further investigation proves that he has good character, that he stands well in his studies and that he really wants to play the game, he is invited for a tryout either at our home park or at some other designated field.

[GETTING YOUR CHANCE]

Examine, if you will, the roster of any major league team and look at the list of home towns from which the active players come, and you will see that the average major league team represents a geographical cross-section of the United States. This should give you some idea of how far away we sometimes go to get a player.

I remember once Ty Cobb was travelling on the West Coast and stopped at the University of California at Berkeley, where a college baseball game was in progress. Cobb was never a man to pass up a ball game anywhere, but I have always been particularly grateful to him for watching that one, because it was on the basis of his telegraphed recommendation after watching the game that the Athletics gave a tryout to Sam Chapman, who has been with us now for a number of years and is one of our valued players.

Only a few days ago I received a tip from a newspaperman who happened to be in Alaska on a journalistic mission. He told me about a nineteen-year-old pitcher in one of the towns up there who, during the season, pitched a couple of one-hitters and a brace of two-hitters. This boy is a native, nineteen years old. According to my newspaper friend he would qualify in every respect, but there developed one slight drawback; he has not yet completed his high school course, not because of any lack of intelligence, but because he got a very late start, there having been no school facilities available in the place where he was born and brought up. But given a chance to complete his education, there is every reason to believe that he will get an opportunity in organized baseball.

On the other hand, it is possible that you may not have

been brought to the attention of a league scout or manager by outside sources of information. The thing for you to do then is to get in touch with the nearest league team in your vicinity, or if you feel that you have that much ability, with the manager of one of the major league clubs.

You must remember that the average duration of a big leaguer's career in active baseball is about ten years. After you reach a certain age you find your legs will not carry you as fast and your co-ordination will not be as speedy as it is when you are younger; then you either shift to a position like coaching or scouting which doesn't require such rigorous physical activity, or you take a job in a minor league in a similar capacity. So the game is constantly requiring new blood and this new blood can come from only one source, youth.

Although in nine cases out of ten the tryout will soon indicate whether you have the ability that is required for professional baseball, it is not the last word. Sometimes a man is rejected at a tryout game who may be picked up by some other team. This has happened in many cases. The same Phil Rizzuto who was credited with having been the spark that set the Yankees afire to win the pennant in 1949 was at one time rejected by the Dodgers when he came up for a tryout.

Now let us assume that you have had a tryout and that some major league manager like myself believes that you have the stuff for big league play. You will not immediately join the roster of the Athletics. From that point on you will have to work your way up to the top just as

[GETTING YOUR CHANCE]

you would in industry, or any other profession that you might choose. There is a ladder which all but a very rarely exceptional player has to climb to reach the top level in major league baseball.

You should be aware of the fact that it isn't an easy life. For a portion of the year you will live away from home; the financial returns do not enable you to live or travel luxuriously, but this is part of the sacrifice that the would-be major league baseball player has to make in order to get to the pinnacle.

Once he has reached the top, if he has the stuff, he can come close to writing his own ticket.

Since the first years of a professional baseball player's career in the game will be spent in the minor leagues, I should like to describe the organization of these leagues in some detail.

I have found that all too little is known about the makeup of these leagues and there is a great deal of misunderstanding about them.

There are at present sixty minor leagues, divided into six principal classifications. They are governed by strict rules; among other things these rules fix the maximum amount of salary which can be paid to the entire team during any one month. The classification of a league, which governs the number of players that each team can have in it at any one time and the maximum aggregate salary that can be paid in any one month, depends on the total population of the cities of the league. The highest classification is Triple A (AAA), in which there are three leagues. There are two Double A (AA) leagues and four A leagues. The remaining fifty-one leagues are divided into B, C and D classifications, twenty-six of them being D leagues.

These minor leagues are organized into a body known as the National Association of Professional Baseball leagues, whose president, George M. Trautman, has his headquarters at Columbus, Ohio. Between the leagues themselves there is what is called the National Association Agreement, but they also have an agreement with the major leagues which is known as the Major-Minor Agreement. While all the leagues are self-governed, and each league has its own constitution, they must abide by the rules set up in the National Association and the Major-Minor Agreements, which take precedence over any rules of the individual league.

Let's start with Class D, which includes such groups as the Blue Ridge, Eastern Shore, Evangeline, Kitty, Sooner State, Tobacco State, Coastal Plain Leagues and others. A Class D league team can pay a maximum total of $2600 a month to its players, who vary from fifteen to seventeen per team in number. That doesn't mean that the player is paid every twelve months in any year. He is paid only for the months in which he actually plays baseball. Quick calculation will show you that this averages about $150 a month per man *during the season.*

We come next to the Class C leagues, which number fifteen, with a maximum of seventeen players and a monthly salary limit aggregating $2800 per team. This classification includes such leagues as the Border, Cotton States, Lone Star, Pioneer, Florida Interna-

[GETTING YOUR CHANCE]

tional, which includes some Cuban teams, and others.

The Class B leagues are considerably better-known and include the Three-I League, the Tri-State, Piedmont, Northeastern and others for a total of nine leagues. Player limit for the B league teams is seventeen and the salary limit is $4000 a month. Still further toward the top is Class A, which contains four leagues, the Central, Eastern, South Atlantic and Western, with a player limit of nineteen and salary limit of $5700 per month per team.

In the Double-A league classification there are two, the Texas League and the Southern Association, each with a nineteen player limit.

The Triple-A group includes the American, International and Pacific Coast Leagues, with a player limit of twenty-three but no salary ceiling.

Teams in all these leagues always start with more players under their control for the first thirty days of the season, but at the end of the first month clubs must cut their rosters down to the limits fixed by the respective league rules.

Most of the minor league teams are made up of young fellows who are just starting their careers in professional baseball. Because of the rigors involved and because for most players in these minor leagues the salaries are low, it takes a chap with strong determination to stick it out. The minor leagues are the testing ground for would-be major leaguers. It is in the Class C and D leagues that the baseball wheat is winnowed from the chaff.

Usually a player who finishes his first year in the C

and D league clubs with credit to himself will find himself raised to a Class B league team or even higher at the end of the season.

If after a year a young player has not been able to earn advancement to a higher-rated league he should consider carefully whether he wants to continue in minor league baseball. Unless some exceptional circumstances have interfered to prevent his getting a real test, he probably lacks the talent and perhaps some of the other qualifications which are required.

That's the beginning. The would-be major leaguer moves up from Class D to Class C then B and A, although it isn't impossible to skip one or even more of the intermediate leagues on the way up.

One of the factors that greatly help the advancement of a player with real ability is the draft. For the protection of the player, the rules of the National Association Agreement provide that after two seasons in baseball, a player on the roster of a Class B, C or D team may be selected by any other club of higher classification. If he has seen service for at least thirty days during each of three seasons and is on a Class A roster, he may be drafted by a team in a higher classification, but to be taken from a Double-A or Triple-A club to a major league club he must have had four seasons in baseball. Thus, a player who has real ability MUST be advanced once he has started up the ladder or else he will be selected by some other club. If he is not advanced and not drafted by another team, he must come to the inescapable conclusion that he has gone as far as he is likely to go in organized baseball. Without this draft rule it would be

[GETTING YOUR CHANCE]

possible for a major league team to "freeze" a good player in the minor leagues and prevent him from getting a major league berth.

Under the draft rules the major league clubs must move a player up within two years or run the risk of having some other team claim him at the draft price.

The draft serves another purpose in that it informs the minor league player what the major league managers think of his ability. If, at the end of two or three years, he has not been moved up and has not been claimed by any of the other higher-rated league teams, it should soon become apparent to him that he is lacking in ability and that perhaps he should find another occupation.

Every major league team has affiliations with a number of minor league teams. At the present time the Athletics are affiliated with fifteen minor league teams including one Triple-A club, two A teams, three B teams, two C teams and seven D teams. Eight of the franchises of these clubs are owned outright by the Athletics and the remaining seven are affiliated with our team through working agreements. A working agreement is a written statement showing a relationship between the two baseball clubs with respect to acquiring players. While the working agreements vary according to the individual circumstances of the clubs involved, in general they give clubs in the higher classifications the privilege of selecting one or more players from the clubs in the lower classification. What would happen is that the Athletics, if they wanted a player on one of the farm teams, would take over a player's contract at a specified sum, but in return would supply the team in the lower classification with players. For example, in the 1950 lineup you will find chaps like Hank Wyse, a pitcher who was drafted from the Shreveport team in the Texas League, and Bob Hooper, a right-hander who won 19 and lost three on the Buffalo team of the International League. The Athletics farm club system, which is under the direction of Arthur H. Ehlers, also our chief scout, consists of the following clubs: Buffalo, New York (Triple A); Savannah, Georgia, and Lincoln, Nebraska (A); Sunbury, Pennsylvania, and Fayetteville, N. Carolina (B); Youngstown, Ohio, and Kewanee, Illinois (C); Portsmouth, Ohio; Red Springs, North Carolina; Tarboro, North Carolina; Lexington, North Carolina; Welch, West Virginia; and Moultrie, Georgia (D). In all, the Athletics now have 342 players in reserve for next season and this is about the average number for any year.

There is no agreement among major league managers as to how many farm clubs a major league team should have or in what classifications they should be. A farm director has to fashion a minor league system to suit the needs of his particular major league team. Some can get along with only eight minor league teams; others require twenty or even more.

The Athletics have tried to regulate the clubs in their minor league setup in such a way as to locate them near sections from which most of their players come. While living near home and playing in the minor leagues a young fellow can cut down his expenses, and since we must confess that the average salaries earned in the minor leagues are not too high, this may help in keeping a chap interested in baseball when the going gets tough.

[GETTING YOUR CHANCE]

I have previously mentioned our scouting staff. In addition to our regular scouts, there are sub-scouts who are affiliated with the minor league clubs. The sub-scout is known as a "bird dog" and he acts as the "eyes" for the regular scout. When he sees a likely prospect, no matter where, he notifies the scout for whom he is operating and the latter takes over from there.

The scouts work directly under the farm director, and the farm director of the Athletics also appoints the managers of all the clubs with which we are connected. Those clubs whose franchises we own also have business managers who are appointed by the farm director.

Every summer the Athletics operate two baseball schools. They serve two excellent purposes in that they help us to discover new talent and spread good-will for our team. However, because we have such a widely scattered farm club system the baseball schools principally cover the Pennsylvania area. But all the other major league teams have adopted the baseball school plan, and any youngster who wants to get instruction in baseball of major league caliber and at the same time find out whether he has the ability required for big league baseball should find out where such a school is being held in his part of the country and take advantage of it by attending.

THE SCOUT
LOOKS YOU OVER

THE first thing a baseball scout asks himself when he watches a prospect is not "Can he play baseball?" but "Can he play baseball according to major league standards?"

There are many other things to be considered but this is the main question. There's a great deal of difference between just playing baseball and playing major league baseball. This difference may not be apparent to a person who has not had big-league experience, but a scout whose profession it is to beat the bushes in search of top-notch talent pretty generally knows at once whether he has a find or not.

The scout looks for three things in a prospect. The first: *Speed*. How fast is he on his feet? Can he run? Are his reactions quick? The second: *The throwing arm*. Can he throw? Far? Fast? Accurately? The third: *Strength*.

[THE SCOUT LOOKS YOU OVER]

Does he have hitting power? Endurance? Can he take it?

These are the things the scout looks for first. If you appear to have all three in a goodly measure, he will make inquiry into your other qualifications. If you lack one, say hitting power, you can still make the grade provided you make up in the strength of your throwing arm for your lack of hitting power, for on that basis you might make a pitcher, or a catcher.

You will generally find, however, that the players who come up to the big leagues *and stay there* are those who possess these three vital qualifications in good measure.

As to the other requirements, the scout first checks a prospect's age. How old is he? Most scouts insist on a minimum age of seventeen years for a rookie. Some few exceptions have become professional baseball players at sixteen, but they have indeed been the exceptions and not the rule. Mel Ott, who was originally a catcher, was one of the exceptions.

Rare indeed is the boy of sixteen who has the strength, endurance and baseball "savvy" to play the professional game. Even the seventeen-year-older is a little young to leave home to go out on the road playing as highly competitive a game as professional baseball.

I would say that except in a very unusual case twenty-two years would be the maximum age for a fellow to start a career in baseball. Remember that he has an apprentice period to go through in the minor leagues and he might be twenty-five or twenty-six before he made the major-league rosters.

The best age at which to start in professional baseball is nineteen, I think.

Now what I have said about starting at the age of nineteen does not hold good for a boy in college. A chap who plays on his college baseball team is really getting the same, or nearly the same, experience that he would get on a minor league team. In addition to his experience, he is getting an education, which is just as important as anything in his life.

I cannot emphasize too strongly my feeling about the importance of education. And there is only one time in your life to obtain a solid education; that is while you are young. Don't go into professional baseball with the idea that you will play the game for a few years, make enough money and then go back to finish your college education. It just isn't done.

True, many a baseball player has been successful in after life even without a college education. I would never take a boy out of college, however, to put him into baseball. I always insist that a young fellow, no matter how promising, finish his college education if he has already started.

The case of Eddie Collins is a case in point. Eddie, who developed into the greatest second baseman in baseball history, in my opinion, was a sophomore at Columbia University when I first heard of him. He originally played shortstop and was also quarterback on the Columbia football eleven, although he only weighed 135 pounds.

My old friends John McGraw, manager of the Giants, and Clark Griffith, manager of the New York Yankees in those days, both knew about Eddie Collins, but they were

[THE SCOUT LOOKS YOU OVER]

afraid he was not heavy enough to make a big-league baseball player.

He was brought to my attention by Billy Lush, who managed a semiprofessional team in upper New York State. In those days a college player could earn money over the summer playing semipro baseball in the vacation belt and not lose his collegiate standing.

Eddie was as fast as lightning, I was told by the scout I sent to look him over. So at the first opportunity, although he still had more than two years to complete his college course, I signed him up.

He continued to play on the Columbia team and was elected captain of the nine in his senior year. In the summer of 1906, I suggested that he go along with the Athletics on their last trip West for the season since his classes didn't start until October 1.

However, not wanting to disclose the fact that he was signed by the Athletics, I listed him as "Eddie Sullivan." His first game with the Athletics was under that name, on September 17, 1906, against the White Sox, who won the pennant that year.

His debut was very auspicious. Batting against Ed Walsh, one of the game's great pitchers, Eddie got one hit in four times at bat. At shortstop he handled seven chances successfully and even stole a base. He played six games with the Athletics that year before going back to college.

Sad to relate, however, they discovered at Columbia that the Lions' captain Collins and my shortstop Sullivan were one identical person. That was the end of Eddie's collegiate baseball career, although he did continue as captain.

The point is, though, that despite the fact that Collins had everything to make him a big-league star, I wouldn't let him quit college to join my team.

Incidentally, I can use Collins as an example of another point I want to make. The position you believe you are best fitted for may not always be the place where you wind up on the team. The scout, or the manager, may see certain abilities in you that you yourself cannot see, skills that would make you more valuable to the team in some other position.

When Collins first joined the Athletics (under his own name, at last) I used him at shortstop for several games. That had been his spot in college baseball and I figured he might do well in the short position for the Athletics. But after watching him very closely, I had some misgivings about his performance at shortstop. I moved him around to third base; that didn't work. Then I put him in right field; that didn't work either.

Then I thought of putting him at second base. My second baseman at the time was Danny Murphy, who had played that position for six years. He was an excellent hitter and very popular with the fans at Shibe Park.

I took a long chance; I moved Danny out to right field and put Eddie Collins on second. The rest is history. Murphy became a much better right fielder than he had ever been a second baseman, and Collins was phenomenal. He was soon right on the heels of Ty Cobb, then the American League's leading hitter, and he was also quite a base-stealer, with 81 stolen bases for the season.

[THE SCOUT LOOKS YOU OVER]

So you see, your first spot on the team is not necessarily your permanent position.

The next thing the scout observes is the prospect's attitude toward the game. There are a number of factors which must be considered when you try to determine a fellow's attitude toward baseball, or for that matter, toward anything in life.

One of these factors is the prospect's competitive spirit. Does he play to win? Does he play as though he were enjoying the game? Is he a good sport?

A big-league player has to have the *will to win*. Some players think this means a constant stream of "pep" talk during a game directed at one's team-mates. I don't. You can't win a ball game by talking victory; *the only way to win is to play to win.*

This doesn't mean fighting with the umpire or baiting him. I respect a fellow more when, on a close one, even though he thinks the decision questionable, he agrees to abide by the decision of the umpire. I have found that in such cases the umpire will realize the play may have been close and will give that player a break on the next questionable decision involving him.

Fighting with the members of the opposing team is not a proper manifestation of the competitive spirit, either. It will get you nowhere except into trouble; in the major leagues fisticuffs on the diamond are sufficient justification for the umpire to send you to the showers. On top of that, you are apt to be fined for misconduct.

Competitive spirit is demonstrated when you are on your toes all the time, playing the game for all it is worth and playing to win. Even though there doesn't seem to be a chance of victory, you won't give up if you have the true competitive spirit. I have seen hundreds of baseball games won by teams that just wouldn't be beaten.

I particularly remember the Boston Braves in the World Series of 1914. *There* was a team that wouldn't be beaten. The Athletics had lost the first two games of the series but the third game (at Boston) looked safely in the bag for us. The score was 2 to 2 at the end of the ninth inning, and the Athletics scored two runs in their half of the tenth. I felt quite secure with a two-run lead because Joe Bush, who was pitching for us, had allowed only five hits.

In the Braves' half of the tenth, Hank Gowdy smashed a home run into the center-field stands; with the next man out, Herb Moran walked and Johnny Evers sent him to third with a screaming single. Moran then scored on a long fly, tying the game up again.

No runs were scored by either team in the eleventh, nor by the Athletics in the opening half of the twelfth. Up came Gowdy again, and with darkness settling over the playing field, he knocked one of Joe Bush's fast ones for a double. Les Mann was put on base to run for Gowdy; the next man up walked and a sacrifice bunt by Moran was picked up by Bush, who thought he had an easy force-out at third on Mann. But Joe's throw to Frank Baker at third went over Baker's head and Mann crossed the plate with the winning run. *There* was a team that *wouldn't be licked!*

Another quality that enters into competitive spirit is *courage*. There are many names for this attribute, but they still come down to the one thing—courage. Courage

[THE SCOUT LOOKS YOU OVER]

is the quality of being able to take it. There are many times in the course of a ball game when you have to be able to take it. As you read on in this book about the way the game is played, this will become more and more evident to you.

One of the elements of courage in baseball is the amount of responsibility you take on yourself. A scout will pay little attention to a prospect who he discovers is always claiming credit for a brilliant play and trying to shift the responsibility for bad plays to his fellow teammates.

Don't give alibis! Don't give phony excuses to try to explain why you did something that let a run come home, or why you missed a catch, or failed to touch a base while rounding it. Most of the time you won't be able to get away with an alibi because your fellow-players will know it is phony.

If you've made a mistake, or a misplay, take the blame for it good-naturedly. You are certainly not going to be hanged, or even put in jail, for missing one—even the greatest of ball players sometimes misses one—and how much more gracious it is to say: "I should have had that one. Sorry," than it is to try to blame someone else for your lapse.

You will gain stature in the eyes of your team-mates if you cheerfully accept the responsibility for those mistakes which should properly be charged against you.

Another factor observed by the scout is the prospect's ambition. Does he really want to get along? Will he try? Or is he lazy? There's no room in major-league baseball for a lazy man, a fellow who wants to let the other fellow do all the hard work and make all the hard catches. No matter how good you may be in all departments of the game, you haven't a chance of making the grade if you're lazy.

Finally, the scout will ask: "What about brains and character?" Don't confuse the two; they are not the same. To get to the top in baseball you need both. The fellow with the ability to think, and to think fast, will forge ahead of the player who makes decisions slowly, because baseball, as it is played today, is a game of quick decisions boldly followed out.

That is one aspect of the game that has changed during the past fifty years. When I first became manager of a big-league team, my players were mostly young men who had been attracted to the game from the sand-lots or the semi-professional teams. It wasn't until after the turn of the century that the college ball-players began to eye baseball as a possible profession. From that time on, from the days of Jack Coombs and Frank Baker and Jack Barry, all of whom played on their respective college teams, and all of whom had college diplomas hanging on their walls, the men who shone in the baseball world were largely men of education.

I recall one outstanding major-leaguer, Moe Berg, who even made Phi Beta Kappa. Believe me, his intellect was no handicap to his play.

Very often a scout, without the knowledge of the prospect, will talk to the latter's teachers or, if he is in college, to his professors, to find out how well he does in his classroom work. When I get a report from a scout on a prospect who is still in school, most of the time an abstract of his school grades and averages is attached to the report.

The scout will also investigate the prospect's character and reputation in his own community. Organized baseball has had embarrassing moments caused by lapses of character on the part of some of its best-known figures at the time.

Consequently, when a player is selected for a major-league team, the manager wants to be assured in advance that he has no bad habits or vices that could have unpleasant effects for either the individual, the team or baseball itself.

In my early days, managers were not so meticulous about the character of a player as they are today. When I first entered the game, some of the professional baseball players of the time were not of the highest caliber. As a matter of fact, in those days many parents objected to their sons' embarking on professional baseball careers because of the type of men they would have to associate with.

That day is gone. We want nobody in major league baseball who cannot stand in the light of the sun as an example, in both private and public life, for the youngsters of the nation to follow.

I remember to this day the time I got my first offer to play professional baseball. It was a very tempting offer and I was anxious to accept it. However, I decided to talk it over with my mother, who was a very wise woman.

That evening we sat down together after supper and I told her I had been offered $90 a month to play for the Meriden, Conn., team. In those days that amount of money was considered a fortune; it was, in fact, twice as much as most of the other players on the team were getting.

Mother knew something about the type of men then playing professional baseball. She pointed out to me that many of them were heavy drinkers; men who thought that the way to win a ball game was with fists and provocative language. If I was determined to accept the offer, however, she said she would not stand in my way.

"I won't ask you to make any promises," were her words to me, "but remember what I tell you now. You'll never get anywhere drinking and fighting."

I have tried to follow her advice and I pass it on to you. In the many years that I have been in the game I have evolved a code of conduct which I follow and to which every good sportsman can subscribe.

Say to yourself:

I will always play the game to the best of my ability.

I will always play to win, but if I lose, I will not look for an excuse to detract from my opponent's victory.

I will never take an unfair advantage in order to win.

I will always abide by the rules of the game—on the diamond as well as in my daily life.

I will always conduct myself as a true sportsman—on and off the playing field.

I will always strive for the good of the entire team rather than for my own glory.

I will never gloat in victory or pity myself in defeat.

[THE SCOUT LOOKS YOU OVER]

I will do my utmost to keep myself clean—physically, mentally and morally.

I will always judge a teammate or an opponent as an individual and never on the basis of his race or religion.

Follow that creed and you will find that it will carry you far not only on the playing field but in anything else you may do in life.

WHAT I LOOK FOR IN
A ROOKIE

EVERY YEAR, about 300 young fellows from every part of the United States, Canada, Cuba, Puerto Rico and many other places are given tryouts by the Athletics. On the basis of recommendations from our scouts and from friends, we invite these aspiring youngsters to come to Philadelphia, or to places where we may be playing, to show us what they have to offer in the way of baseball talent.

Quite a number of these youngsters get the break they are looking for; they may be sent to one of our farm clubs or, if they are exceptionally good, they may be invited to join the team in spring training.

Now every one of these would-be major-leaguers is a different personality; each one has some marked ability in a definite direction that has led someone familiar with

[WHAT I LOOK FOR IN A ROOKIE]

big league baseball to believe that he might make the grade.

It is my job, with the team's coaches and the scouts, to decide which of the candidates is to go further—at least as far as the Athletics are concerned. And it is also my job, one that I do not relish as much as some others, to tell the boys who don't make the grade that we can't use them.

More often than not, the fellows who are to pack up and go home don't ask why they haven't been chosen. They seem to realize that they need more training or experience or that in competition with the elite of major league baseball they would not quite come through.

Every once in a while, though, a young chap will ask: "What's wrong with me? Just what are you looking for in a rookie?"

Well, that's a good question and one that deserves to be answered for the benefit of all the boys of America who aspire to the ranks of the exalted 400 players who comprise the 16 major league teams.

Every manager has his own standards but generally we all look for the same things in a fellow who wants to play on our teams. We recognize that no individual rookie will be perfect, or even outstanding, in every qualification, but what he lacks in one department, say the ability to field a ball quickly, he may compensate for in another, perhaps by being a terrific hitter.

We take it for granted that when a scout recommends a player to us for a tryout, he has baseball ability. When he gets the tryout, his baseball talent is tested, of course. But there are other elements which are observed at the same time.

Here is the answer to the question. These are the things *I* look for in a rookie:

> Physical ability
> Intelligence
> Courage
> Disposition
> Will power
> General alertness
> Personal habits

As I have said, one man can't possess every one of these qualifications to the highest degree. If he did, and he could play baseball well, he would probably be the super-baseball player of all time. You see, there are many things that go on behind the scenes of baseball that the average baseball fan knows nothing about, involving the personalities of players. In my two-thirds of a century of association with baseball, I have known many, many wonderful players; I have, however, still to meet the perfect baseball player. Frankly, I don't think he exists.

In grading a prospect, it is only fair to gauge him on all points, so that if he runs a little high on some factors, the extra ability will be taken into account if there are any deficiencies elsewhere.

A good example of what I mean is in the size of the player. My preference would be for a big strapping fellow who can run and throw and hit with equal skill. I think

[WHAT I LOOK FOR IN A ROOKIE]

every other manager would go for the big chaps, too. Baseball can be somewhat rugged in spots, particularly where endurance counts, and there size and muscle pay off.

Most of the power hitters have been big men: Babe Ruth tipped the scales at more than 200 pounds; Hank Greenberg stands six feet five and has a playing weight of 200 pounds or more. Jimmy Foxx, who could hit a home run farther than anyone else I ever saw, was not only big, but heavy, too.

But that doesn't mean a smaller fellow can't be a great baseball player. Take Mel Ott, who played 22 years in the major leagues. He weighed about 165 pounds at playing weight and stood five feet nine inches or so, but during his career he poled out a total of 511 home runs. Not bad for a little fellow.

So, although I prefer size, I am willing to take a smaller man if he has added ability to compensate for his lack of brawn. That doesn't mean the smaller fellow doesn't have to have a certain amount of physical strength. He does. He has to have a strong throwing arm, power enough in his batting arm to hit the ball squarely and hard; he has to have fleetness of foot for fielding and running the bases; he has to have a good, strong, sure pair of hands and good eyesight.

Almost instinctively, among the first things I look at when I am introduced to a prospect are his hands. You would be surprised to know what a manager learns about a young ball player just by watching him use his hands. I watch to see how he picks up a grounder, how he catches a fly ball and how he grips his bat.

If he has a strong, agile pair of hands through which the strength of his muscles can flow, you may be fairly sure that he is a natural baseball player.

To make the grade in the major leagues you have to be able to hit hard, throw hard and run fast. Fundamentally, these are things you can't learn to do. Either you start with them or you don't. Good coaching can help you hit the ball harder, or throw it farther, or even to run faster. But take the fast pitch, for example. You can't learn to throw a fast ball as you can learn to throw a curve or a change of pace. Either you have it to start with or you don't.

Or take batting. Some players are extraordinary batters from the start. Others have what it takes—good rhythm, keen eyesight and excellent co-ordination of muscles. But they don't combine the factors properly to make the fullest use of them. Good coaching can help these players improve their batting ability. Sometimes it requires only a simple little change in stance, or standing closer to or farther away from the plate.

Jimmy Foxx was a good example of this. Although he led the American League in batting averages several years, Jimmy was a rather mediocre hitter when he first came to the Athletics. But anyone looking at that broad-shouldered build and those powerful arm muscles could see that he had the makings; what he needed was coaching. After he got it—well, you know what happened.

The next thing I look for in a rookie is intelligence, or the ability to apply his mind to the game. I don't know how the tradition ever got started that baseball players were short on brains. That just isn't so. There is nothing

[WHAT I LOOK FOR IN A ROOKIE]

in life that takes the place of education, not even experience, and every manager would prefer a rookie with a college education. Some of the most famous players I've had on my teams in the last fifty years have been college men.

Chief Albert Bender, who still coaches the Athletics, was a student at Carlisle Indian School when I first heard of him. Incidentally, Jim Thorpe, one of the greatest athletes who ever lived, also came from the same school. Eddie Plank, who is now enshrined in Baseball's Hall of Fame, played for Gettysburg College before joining the A's. Eddie Collins, another of baseball's greatest stars, played on the Columbia University varsity nine before signing up with the Athletics.

Sam Chapman, who is a member of the present Athletics, came from the University of California, where, by the way, he was also an All-American football player.

Baseball is not a mechanical game. It is a game of strategy. It calls for planning and thinking. It calls for a study of the opposing players, their weaknesses and personal peculiarities. I've seen many a game won because a player was smart enough to remember a single little detail about another player's habit and take advantage of it.

Brains are as important in baseball as they are in every other endeavor. I would never encourage a young man to leave college to sign a contract with a baseball club. If he's that good, there will still be an opening for him after he has got his diploma.

A young fellow named Bill McCahan, brought to my attention by his uncle, once played with the Athletics.

At the time, Bill was going to high school in a little town near Philadelphia. It was a shame, I felt, for Bill to give up a chance to get a college education, but I also felt he had the makings of a good pitcher.

I suggested to Bill that he finish his high school course and then enroll at Duke University in North Carolina, where my old-time "Iron Man" pitcher, Jack Coombs, is baseball coach. Bill did very well at Duke, and Coombs taught him the fine art of pitching, so well that in Bill's first year with the Athletics—of course, we signed him up—he pitched a no-hit, no-run game against the Washington Senators.

The third thing I look for in a would-be baseball star is courage. A man can have all the physical power in the world, but power by itself is not the equivalent of courage. No player ever reached the pinnacle in baseball without courage. It takes courage to stand at the plate against a fast ball pitcher. It takes courage to slam into a concrete wall or an iron fence trying to catch a fly ball or a foul.

It takes courage to slide into second base or third with a faceful of spikes waiting for you and a hard-thrown ball flying at your head. It takes courage to try to steal home with the catcher, generally a rock of a man, waiting for you. It takes courage to go back on the playing field again, or to stand up to the plate, after you've been beaned by a pitched ball. Baseball, as it is played for keeps in the major leagues, is not a sissy game; it takes courage.

I have known many examples of courage on the baseball field, but there's one that stands out in my mind

[WHAT I LOOK FOR IN A ROOKIE]

above all others. I have a young pitcher on my present Athletics team by the name of Lou Brissie. When he was a youngster the great dream of his life was to be a major league pitcher, and when the war came, he was well on his way to realizing his ambition.

However, into the Army he went and he was assigned to duty overseas. He took part in the campaign in Italy, and in one of the battles over there a shell exploded in the midst of an infantry detachment in which he was serving.

They took Lou to a hospital and found that his left leg had been severely wounded. The surgeons told him that if he wanted to live, they would have to amputate the leg.

"Oh, no," said Lou. "You can't take my leg off. I'm going to need it to play baseball."

Well, they didn't take it off. It took more than twenty surgical operations to bring Lou to the point where he could use the leg at all. He now wears a plastic-and-aluminum plate around his left leg; if you look at the photograph of him in this book you will notice that he wears the leg of his uniform pants down around the ankle to cover the protective plate.

Early in the 1948 schedule, the Athletics played the Red Sox at Shibe Park in Philadelphia. In the course of the game, Lou had to pitch to Ted Williams. Ted took a couple of pitches and then laid into one of Brissie's fast ones. The ball shot from the end of the bat like a bullet out of a gun and, traveling on a direct line, hit Lou's injured leg.

Brissie dropped like a felled ox. I think my heart must have stopped beating. I thought to myself: "That poor boy! That's the end of his baseball career." Ted Williams and everybody else in the park must have felt the same way.

Time was called and the Athletics' trainer went out to the pitching mound. After a few agonizing minutes, the word came back that Lou had not been hurt but the aluminum plate was badly dented. I wanted to send in another pitcher to replace Brissie, but he said "No."

He not only finished the game—and won it, too,—but when Williams came to bat the next time around, Lou faced him firmly and STRUCK HIM OUT! THAT took a lot of courage, in my opinion.

Another thing I look for in a rookie is a pleasant disposition. A man has to have a sociable disposition to play in the major leagues. He has to be able to get along with his teammates and his manager. He has to be able to take orders, for the manager's instructions are the last word in playing a baseball game. He also has to be able to take criticism without grumbling.

I like a fellow who, when he has made a misplay, is good enough sport to say: "That was MY fault," instead of trying to alibi himself off the spot and put another fellow on it. That not only will gain him the respect of his fellow-players but will bolster his own self-respect as well. And it will make him a better baseball player in the end.

Sometimes—not too often, fortunately—a chap gets the idea that he can play his own game. But such a fellow doesn't usually last in the major leagues. He soon learns that baseball is a game played by a team, and that no individual player is bigger than the team.

A ballplayers' ballplayer is the fellow who constantly works for the team and its success, and if he has to sacrifice to advance a teammate around the bases, why, that's all right, too. If the manager thinks someone else may do better in a pinch, the big-leaguer has to be ready and willing to step aside at any time.

As I have said, the element of discipline enters into the game when the manager gives orders. A player MUST follow the orders given by the bench, no matter what he thinks of the strategy employed.

There is a story told about Babe Ruth that demonstrates what I mean. I must admit that I never got the story first hand, but it is often told around the circuit, and it is a splendid illustration of the point I am trying to make.

Babe was at bat one day for the Yankees, with no one out and a man on first. The great swatter was feeling his best and as he stood at the plate with that look of confidence on his face that he always wore when he was in the pink, he seemed to be saying to the pitcher: "Come on, put it in here and I'll murder it!"

Then came the signal from the bench for a bunt in the hope of advancing the man on first to second at the cost of one out. The first pitch was too low for him to get, but on the second toss he took the kind of swipe at the ball that only Babe Ruth could take. Smack! High into the air it sailed and far away—for a home run.

The Babe followed his teammate across the plate and the Yankees were two runs to the good. The crowd cheered and his teammates shook Ruth's hand as he trotted over to the bench.

Manager Joe McCarthy was waiting for him. "That'll cost you a hundred bucks," he said grimly.

"A hundred bucks?" squealed the Babe. "What's the the big idea?"

"Just this," answered McCarthy. "When I give an order on this team, I want it followed. And that goes for *you*, too, understand?"

The Babe understood, all right. He followed orders from that time on.

The next qualification I look for in a rookie is his will power. A real ballplayer has to be able to stay in there when the going is tough. A pitcher may have a fine mound job ruined by an outfielder's error, but he still has to keep bearing down.

I well remember a game back in 1924 when the Athletics were playing Cleveland in Philadelphia. Pitching for us was Stan Baumgartner, who had played varsity baseball at the University of Chicago. Stan, by the way, is now a top-notch sports writer for the *Philadelphia Inquirer* and often accompanies the Athletics on training trips and tours away from home during the regular season.

At any rate, the Indians hit everything Stan threw at them that day. They would have hit the water bucket for safeties if Stan had thrown it. It was clearly not one of his good days, so I took him out of the box and sent him to the showers. In his place I sent in Eddie Rommel.

In the eighth, Cleveland was leading, 13 to 2. I got the impression that Eddie wasn't bearing down, figuring there was no hope of winning the game, so when he came to the bench I said to him: "Eddie, no matter what the score is, I want you to bear down. You can never tell what's going to happen in a ball game."

[WHAT I LOOK FOR IN A ROOKIE]

The words were hardly out of my mouth when the Athletics started a batting rally that was incredible, scoring 14 runs in the eighth. The final score was Athletics 16, Cleveland 14.

By the time all this had happened, Baumgartner was at his home, having left the park after dressing. He was watering his lawn and had moved a portable radio set out on his front porch to follow the closing innings. He turned the radio on just in time to hear the announcer say: ". . . and the Athletics lead, 16 to 14."

Stan was certain that someone was playing a practical joke on him. And he wouldn't believe the score until I assured him over the telephone that the broadcaster was telling the truth.

The Athletics had another situation like that in the fourth game of the 1929 World Series against the Chicago Cubs. Two of my pitchers had been riddled and the same Eddie Rommel was trying in vain to hold the Cubs. At the end of the first half of the seventh the score stood 8 to 0 in favor of the Cubs.

I had made up my mind to take the first-stringers out and put in a whole team of substitutes at the beginning of the eighth. Charlie Root, in the box for the Cubs, had held the Athletics to three scattered hits when Al Simmons came to bat leading off the second half of the "stretch" inning.

Bam! Simmons connected for a homer to the roof of the left-field stand. I remember Jimmy Dykes, who was sitting next to me on the bench, muttering consolingly: "Well, we won't be shut out anyway."

Next in the batting order were Jimmy Foxx, Bing

[CONNIE MACK'S BASEBALL BOOK]

Miller and Jimmy Dykes himself. Each of them touched Root for a single, and Foxx scored. Joe Boley was next up. I told him to swing at the first good one. It looked to me as though Root was fading.

Boley knocked out a single, and Miller scored. I sent in George Burns as a pinch hitter for Rommel, but Burns popped out. The score was 8 to 3, with one out and two men on base.

Max Bishop rekindled the fire with another single and Dykes scooted around scoring our fourth run. That was all for Root. Art Nehf, a one-time Giant southpaw, took his place. The first batter to face him was Mule Haas, who drove a scorcher to center.

Apparently blinded by the sun, Hack Wilson, the Cubs' center-fielder, let the ball get away from him and before the Chicago left fielder had chased it and thrown it in, Boley and Bishop had crossed the rubber and Haas was tearing around third headed for the plate, too.

I leaned forward to watch Haas slide. The play was very close and very exciting and when the dust had cleared and the plate umpire indicated Haas was safe, Jimmy Dykes, who had resumed his seat next to me in the dugout, slapped me on the back in his great excitement. Seated on the edge of the bench as I had been, the slap sent me sprawling among the bats. But I didn't mind, under the circumstances.

The score was now 8 to 7 against us. After Mickey Cochrane, the next batter, had walked, Manager Joe McCarthy yanked Nehf and substituted Blake. The first two batters to face him, Simmons and Foxx, batting for

[WHAT I LOOK FOR IN A ROOKIE]

the second time, each rapped out singles again, tying the score at 8–all.

Out went Blake and in came Pat Malone, whose first pitch struck Bing Miller in the ribs; the bases were filled with only one man out. Next man up was Jimmy Dykes. He was aiming to hit a long fly to bring in another run from third, but he didn't know his own strength. The ball travelled beyond the reach of Stephenson in left field and went for a double, with Simmons and Foxx parading across the plate again. The score: Athletics 10, Chicago Cubs 8. The next two men were easy outs for Malone.

That turned out to be the final score, for Bob Grove, who went in to take Rommel's place, was really "hot." He retired the next six Chicago players in order, striking out four of them.

No, you can never tell what's going to happen in a ball game.

Whenever I watch a rookie I look to see whether he is alert, on his toes all the time. Is he on the move every minute, hustling and trying for anything and everything? Does he play it out, or does he give up if he seemingly can't make the play?

Remember this: You can't get them if you don't try.

What every manager wants is a player who is in there trying all the time, never letting up. Major league baseball is no game for a lazy body or a lazy mind. Many a player has made the grade because he impressed the manager as a hustler when he got his tryout or during his trial period.

Such a player was Mickey Cochrane, who was not only

a very great catcher but also a real dynamo on the field. The Athletics acquired Mickey in 1924, the same year we bought Lefty Grove for what was then the highest price ever paid for a player, $100,000. Actually, to get Cochrane we bought the Portland club of the Pacific Coast League.

It isn't often that you buy a whole club just to get one player but I've never regretted that purchase. I'd gladly buy another club to get another Mickey Cochrane.

One of the things that I insist on is that a rookie who is going to play with my team must have good moral habits and self-control. You can have everything else that's needed to make the grade, but if you don't have a good moral character, you are not for the major leagues.

A good ballplayer takes care of himself for his own sake and for the team's sake. Baseball clubs never spend any money buying players with bad reputations off the field, and believe me, every candidate for a major league team gets a good going over by way of preliminary investigation before he's finally signed up.

A manager can't have faith in a man who, when needed in an emergency, shows up in no condition to play. Elsewhere in this book I have mentioned the great Rube Waddell, who played for the Athletics in the early 1900's. Rube was a marvelous player, but he was not dependable.

He liked to look on the wine when it was red, and as a result, no matter how great he was at times, he wouldn't be tolerated on a big-league team today.

One of today's synonyms for success is the expression: "He's made the big leagues." That means a man has

[WHAT I LOOK FOR IN A ROOKIE]

gone to the top. It's a safe bet that when people say of a man that "he's made the big leagues," he's a dependable fellow.

Self-control comes under this heading, too. A manager likes a fellow to be scrappy, to have the will to win, but that doesn't mean he has to get into continual arguments with the umpires or into fisticuffs with members of the opposing team.

I have great respect for the big league umpires. I find very few occasions to argue with their decisions and I tell my players that they should abide by their decisions, too. I must admit that sometimes a player's feelings, in the heat of the game, get to be too much for him and he has to let off steam, so that the umpire becomes a target.

But don't think that you make much of an impression on a manager by fighting with an umpire. If anybody is going to fight with the umpire, let the manager do it, or the team captain.

And now for the last, but not the least important item in the make-up of a desirable rookie—self-confidence under fire. That doesn't mean brashness or show-offishness. It means the kind of stuff that Howard Ehmke showed in that World Series of 1929 against the Cubs.

That Cubs team was an aggregation of super-hitters; among them were Rogers Hornsby, Kiki Cuyler, Hack Wilson, Woody English and Charlie Grimm.

Howard Ehmke was then 35 years old, nearing the end of his pitching career. During the 1929 season he had pitched only two complete games, with none-too-good results.

Just before the Athletics left on their last Western trip

of the season, I called Howard into my office in the tower of Shibe Park. "Howard," I said, "there comes a time in everyone's life when there has to be a change. I'm afraid we're soon going to have to part company."

"That's all right, Mr. Mack," he replied. "If that's the way it is, that's the way it has to be. I haven't helped you much this year, and it's lucky you haven't needed me. But I've always wanted to pitch in a World Series, and if this is my last season, I'd like to work in this one, maybe only for a couple of innings."

Howard flexed his muscle and said, confidently: "I think I've got one more good game in there."

"So do I," I told him. I instructed him to stay in the East while the team went West and to watch the Cubs when they played the Phillies and the Giants. "See what they like to hit," I advised, "and make notes on them. Don't say anything to anyone, but I'm going to pitch you in the first game of the Series."

Well, the night before the Series opened at Wrigley Field, Chicago, I named Ehmke as my starting pitcher. Nobody believed it. Everyone in baseball believed he was through. When Howard started to warm up, the sports writers were asking each other whether I was in my right mind.

Ehmke himself didn't realize what a game he had tucked away in that arm of his. The Athletics won, 3 to 1; Howard struck out 13 men that afternoon for a new World Series record. The Cubs didn't score until the ninth when Jimmy Dykes threw a wild one. Had it not been for that throw, I believe Ehmke would have shut the Cubs out.

[WHAT I LOOK FOR IN A ROOKIE]

That's the kind of self-confidence I mean. I got a great thrill that afternoon in Chicago, watching a fellow who knew this was probably his last game in the major leagues. But he had enough confidence in himself to believe he could win, even against the hardest-hitting ball club of the National League.

As long as baseball is played and great performances are remembered, that terrific effort of Howard Ehmke will be a shining example for all would-be major league players.

WHICH POSITION
DO YOU WANT TO PLAY?

BASEBALL CAN be a lifetime profession.

Any young fellow considering a career in professional baseball should start with that proposition.

Too often a college player with talent accepts a contract to play on a professional team with the mental reservation that he is only filling in an interval; that he will stay in professional baseball for a few years until something more attractive comes along.

That's the wrong approach. A chap who starts, let us say, at twenty-two after graduating from college doesn't attain his full baseball maturity for five or six years. That makes him about twenty-seven. He stays at the peak of his game for another five or six years, which take him to thirty-three.

From then on he still may have a few years of active play left in his legs and arms; after they've been used up

[WHICH POSITION DO YOU WANT TO PLAY?]

he still has remaining the greatest asset in baseball: the "know-how" of the game.

He can be used as a coach, or a scout, in the "front office" or in one of many other capacities where all the accumulated experience of his years in baseball will be of great value.

Then, too, I have found that baseball is loyal to its own. Unless there is a mighty compelling reason against it, organized baseball generally finds some niche for those who have helped to improve the game and have added to its luster, even when they no longer have the speed and endurance required for actual play.

If you do not intend to make your baseball career a lifetime job you should consider carefully whether you want to start in it at all. When you make up your mind that baseball is IT, you should then consider which position on the team you want to fill. You will learn, as you read on in this book, that different activities on the diamond require different physical characteristics. There are some positions that a little fellow can fill satisfactorily; there are others that are open principally to the big fellows. Any little fellow who makes the grade in the major leagues, however, must have ability *plus*.

This is what I consider the ideal physique for a major-league player: Height: from five feet ten inches to six feet. Weight: 175 to 185 pounds. Body build in proportion.

I don't mean to say that if you're five feet eight or nine and only weigh 165 pounds there's no place for you in major league baseball. But unless you are the rare exception your opportunity would be limited. It would be extremely difficult, for example, to be a pitcher or catcher with the lesser qualifications.

At the same time, bigness by itself isn't enough. A prospect who is too big is as much handicapped as a prospect who is not big enough. The oversized fellow is very often too awkward and unable to break away quickly enough for either fielding or base running.

If a player is below the ideal height and weight qualifications I have stated but is so good in all departments that you can't keep him off the team, the best place to put him is in the infield. The oversized fellows you find mostly in either the pitcher's or catcher's spot or on first base. None of these three positions calls for much fielding that requires a speedy foot; in any of these spots if a player excels in other respects I would be willing to forgo a little speed.

Everywhere else on the diamond, however, speed is essential and there I prefer a fast man, particularly a fast-breaking runner. In the kind of baseball that is played today, many a base runner is either out or safe by a single step.

Which is more important, height or weight? I would say *weight*. While a not-so-tall player usually has short legs and short arms and is therefore handicapped in fielding and batting, if he is muscular and strong he still has the edge over the too-tall player whose height makes him awkward and who is virtually helpless against low pitches.

Except in the pitcher's box, I prefer a short, sturdy player with muscular strength and the endurance that as a rule goes along with it to a tall thin fellow whose ability

[WHICH POSITION DO YOU WANT TO PLAY?]

to play a regulation nine-inning game at peak activity may be questionable.

Your throwing arm will have a great deal to do with your position on the team. The pitcher, obviously, must have the finest throwing arm on the team; that is to say, he must have speed, control and variety. You can read more of this in detail in the chapter on pitching.

The next best throwing arm on the team ought to belong to the shortstop. Of all the fielders he has to be fast on the throw and accurate. Following him in the order in which a good throwing arm is essential are the first baseman, then the third baseman, who sometimes has to field a bunted ball and get it away to first base.

Now the ability to throw a ball fast or far is of itself not enough. Speed and distance don't count for much if they do not have accuracy to go with them. A long throw that doesn't come near its intended mark or a fast throw that goes wide of its target may cost more, in terms of the score, than if the ball had not been fielded at all.

Accuracy in throwing calls for control and co-ordination. Very often the fielder will not have time to get "set" for the throw after he has caught or stopped the ball. He must be "set" before he receives it. The catcher, for example, is set for his throw the instant the ball leaves the pitcher's hand.

In playing both infield and outfield, a lot of attention should be paid to footwork; upon fielding a ball, the player should be in position to throw to any base involved without taking more than one step. Remember this: for every step taken by a fielder before he throws the ball for the play at the base, the runner is taking a step, too. So in addition to everything else, the base runner is in effect running a footrace with the fielder.

A thrown ball will reach its mark more quickly if it is thrown on a line and is not lobbed or curved. Throw the ball to the player who is to receive it so that he can take it in the best and most convenient position for the play he is trying to make. For example, if he is a baseman and a runner is heading for his base, the ball should reach him low so that he will not have to move far to tag the runner. A long throw from the outfield should come in on the bounce; it will be easier to handle that way.

I have spoken about throwing the ball; before you can throw it you must have caught it. To catch a ball well, a player has to have big hands. You will also find this subject treated at length in a later chapter; let me say at this point only that in order to catch the ball you have to get to it. That's where the element of speed comes in, speed and judgment of the ball's flight, because you must estimate where it will fall and how you can best get there before it.

Whether the ball is in the air or on the ground, there is one fundamental fielding rule to be followed by a baseball player who hopes to play professionally: Get *behind* the ball and *stay there*. After you have got behind it, keep your eye on the ball until it is in your glove.

And you must always be *ready* for the ball. You never know, in the course of a game, when the ball is going to be hit to you. You should therefore be prepared to field the ball on every pitch because that might be the one the batter sends in your direction.

That brings up the question of physical suppleness. In-

[WHICH POSITION DO YOU WANT TO PLAY?]

fielders particularly should be supple and loose-jointed. A stiff-jointed player will not be able to retrieve a "shoe-stringer." Very often a player has to dive head first to made a catch or leap high in the air for the ball. A man who is anchored to the ground cannot do this.

Remember that the opposing side will never purposely hit the ball to you. In fact, its purpose will be to hit the ball where you "ain't," to paraphrase a baseball maxim ascribed to Wee Willie Keeler. But no matter where it may be hit, your purpose should be to get it into your hands. This failing, you should at all costs attempt to stop it, for if it gets past you, it may cost your team a run, perhaps more.

This is emphatically true in the outfield. The outfielders have at least one advantage over the infielders: They have more time to judge the course of the ball after it has been hit and they also have more time to get behind the ball. For that reason, there is less excuse for an error by an outfielder than a similar fault by an infielder.

One of the finest outfielders I have known was Ty Cobb. He is written down in baseball history for many other accomplishments: I do not believe that he has been given full credit for his achievements as a fielder. Cobb was a real "ball hawk." He knew, somehow, at the instant the pitcher let go of the ball where it was going to be hit, and times without number he would move to the spot in time for the catch when there was no earthly reason for him to be there.

He had a peculiar way of catching a fly ball which hasn't been duplicated and which I would not recommend to anyone else; I doubt if anyone but Cobb could do the trick. On a fly, Cobb wouldn't look at the ball. He would look down at the ground and catch the ball directly over his head without even looking. Ty was very much misunderstood by many fans around the country but there is no player in the history of the game who excelled him in all-round ability.

Self-confidence counts for a great deal in major-league baseball. A player who does not have self-confidence will not rise to stardom. You have to feel that you have what it takes and you have to feel it very deeply. Now that calls for one of the most difficult requirements of all: the faculty of being able to appraise yourself and your ability TRUTHFULLY and HONESTLY.

It is not hard for any of us to think of ourselves as we would like to be. This is sometimes referred to as "wishful thinking." You can easily *imagine* yourself another Alvin Dark or a Richie Ashburn, a rookie of the year. But if you sit down and search for the honest-to-goodness answers to the vital questions, can you really be honest with yourself?

Self-confidence stems from knowing just what you *can* do and what you *cannot* do. It is well to remember that your faults will stand out all the more if they are exposed in the pinch. So will your extra good qualities and abilities.

As I have said, you very seldom find a big-league ball player who doesn't have real self-confidence. One of the best examples of self-confidence in a baseball player, I think, was Babe Ruth. In his physical build he was nearly everything, I guess, that a baseball player should not be.

[**WHICH POSITION DO YOU WANT TO PLAY?**]

He had a big body; he weighed more than 200 pounds. His legs were thin. Sometimes when you watched him at bat you wondered how his thin legs could support his big body, much less carry it around the field or around the bases. But the Babe was supremely confident of himself no matter what the situation was.

In the third game of the 1932 World Series, the Yankees were playing against the Cubs at Wrigley Field in Chicago. Ruth was at bat; Charlie Root burned a fast one over the plate and the Babe took a terrific cut at it. He missed, and so vicious was his swing that he twisted completely around on the follow-through and wound up sitting in the dirt in the batter's box.

Every one of the thousands of spectators in the park laughed heartily, myself included. But the Babe wasn't abashed. He picked himself up from the ground, dusted off his uniform and stepped back into the batter's box. On his face was that unforgettable grin of his.

Facing Charlie Root, he pointed the bat in the direction of the center field stands. He said nothing in words but you couldn't mistake his meaning. His gesture spoke the words for him: "I'm going to knock the next pitch into the center field stands." And by golly! that's just what he *did* do. He hit the next pitch for a home run, and the ball went directly where he indicated it would.

THAT was a demonstration of self-confidence that will long be remembered and the fans were not long in showing their appreciation of this remarkable feat.

The Babe's called home run was not the first time, however, that a major-league player had made good on a promise to hit a specific pitch for a four-bagger. Ty Cobb did it in the early 1920's on a pitch off Walter Johnson when the Detroit Tigers were playing the Washington Senators one day at Washington.

It was at Washington that a batter called a pitch for a home run for the first time in the major leagues and because the incident had a humorous side, I should like to tell you about it.

During the 1909 season, there was a player on the Washington team by the name of Herman Shaeffer, better known to players and fans of the time as "Germany" Shaeffer because of the country of his nativity and his accent. He was a fellow of infinite good humor, always joking and never discouraged but withal a player of very high ability. That season had not been one of the best for either Germany Shaeffer or the Washington team.

In this particular game, Washington was behind 13 to 2 as the home team came to bat in the last half of the ninth inning. With two men out and nobody on base, Shaeffer came to the plate.

Just to get a laugh out of the overwhelming defeat, Shaeffer left the batter's box and went to the edge of the Senators' dugout where Manager Joe Cantillon was getting ready to call it a day.

"What shall I do now?" asked Shaeffer in a voice loud enough to be heard in the bleachers.

"Why, you big lop-eared ape!" shouted back Manager Cantillon, somewhat angry at Shaeffer's idea of a joke. "You're supposed to hit the first ball pitched over the right field fence. That's what you're supposed to do."

Shaeffer went back to the plate and held up his hand

[WHICH POSITION DO YOU WANT TO PLAY?]

for silence as he faced the fans still remaining in the stands.

"Ladies and gentlemen," he began. "I have been ordered to hit the ball over the right field fence. A good ball player always follows orders," he said with mock seriousness. "I will therefore hit the ball over the right field fence."

He stood up to the first pitch and wham! over the right field fence it went. Incidentally, that was Germany Shaeffer's *only home run* during the 1909 season.

In any position you play on the team you must be alert, ready for anything that may happen. The unexpected is always happening in baseball; that's what makes it such a fascinating game. If you are always prepared for the unexpected, you will be able to capitalize on the breaks and thus give your team an advantage.

There is on record an instance of a ball that had been hit out of the park having been caught for a put-out because an outfielder was on the alert. It was one of those unexpected things that can happen to change the whole complexion of a ball game.

Walter Johnson, the Washington Senators' great pitcher, who was nicknamed "Big Train," was not only a star on the mound, but he was no pushover at bat, either. On this particular day the Senators were playing the White Sox and Johnson, getting a pitch he liked, sent it screaming over the center-field fence for what was apparently a home run.

Out in center field, Johnny Mostil, the White Sox outfielder, saw the ball go sailing over his head. He followed it with his eyes as it passed beyond the fence. After travelling a few feet, however, the ball was met by a gust of wind which braked its flight and carried it so far back that it fell into the park.

Now Mostil would have been justified in turning around and facing the diamond once he saw the ball go over the fence. But Johnny was on his toes. He didn't turn around right away. He was surprised, all right, to see the ball coming back into the park—but he was also prepared. He caught the ball before it touched the ground.

There was quite an argument when the umpire ruled that Johnson was out on a legally caught fly. Even though it had passed beyond the limits of the playing field, the umpire decided the ball had not passed out of sight, and as long as it was in sight, it was playable.

It might not happen again in twenty years; the point is that when it DOES happen, in the big leagues you have to be ready for it, as Johnny Mostil was.

Although you will learn that a player nearly always gets instructions from the bench or the coaches, every once in a while a manager will tell a player to use his own judgment on a play. I have found this a good way to banish nervousness in a particular player and build up his confidence in himself.

This incident goes back a long way, but in the 1913 World Series against the Giants, I used a young fellow as my catcher who had not had too much major league experience up to that time. He was Wally Schang, later to become one of the best backstops in the League. This was his first World Series.

Schang was somewhat nervous and sat pretty close to

[WHICH POSITION DO YOU WANT TO PLAY?]

me on the bench when he was not actually behind the plate. Jack Barry was on first when Wally came to bat. Schang looked at me. "What shall I do, Mr. Mack?" he asked.

"Anything you want," I answered. "You just go out there and do anything you want."

Wally tried to bunt the first ball pitched, but it went foul. Before the second pitch, he gave the hit-and-run sign to Barry, who took a lead off first. The Giants' second baseman ran over to the bag to cover his base while Schang hit the ball right into the hole left by the second baseman when he ran back to the base.

It was Schang's own idea and when he got back to the bench, I complimented him on it. I think that move did more than anything else to get rid of the jitters that a fellow naturally has when he plays in the World Series for the first time.

Just a word of advice: If you want to make good in *any* league, have confidence in yourself and use your head.

THE BATTER

I GUESS there are more misconceptions about batting than about any other department of baseball.

The greatest misbelief is that expression you hear so often: "Good batters are born, not made."

It's not so. Given a fellow who is an average, or even below-average hitter, but who has the natural requirements of a good hitter, an understanding coach or manager can make a first-class batsman out of him. It's been done time and time again.

I'm going to tell you what those natural requirements are. If you have them, you have the stuff of which big-league batters are made. They are: 1: Good vision. 2: The right stance. 3: The right stride. 4: The right swing.

In my fifty years as manager of the Athletics I have had some of baseball's greatest hitters on my team, fel-

[THE BATTER]

lows like Jimmy Foxx, who is runner-up to Babe Ruth in the number of home runs hit in a season, and Al Simmons and Sam Chapman. And on opposing teams I have been up against opponents like the Babe himself, Ted Williams, Joe DiMaggio, Ty Cobb and Lou Gehrig.

So I have had plenty of opportunity to discern the difference between the run-of-the-league batters and those whose names go down in the all-time records.

You will find that difference in the four points I have set out above. You may as well know at the outset: If you want to make the major leagues, you MUST be able to hit. In every department other than pitching, you may be a phenomenal wonder, but if you can't hit, you won't make the grade.

Let's review some of the mathematics of baseball. Although one team is spoken of as opposing another, when a batter is at the plate it's actually one man against nine. The batter is trying to hit safely; the pitcher and his eight team-mates are trying to prevent him from doing so.

The distance between the pitcher and the batter—between the mound and the plate—is 60 feet 6 inches, and across this distance the pitcher throws the ball, which is not quite three inches in diameter, at a speed of close to 100 miles an hour.

Yes, that's right—nearly 100 miles an hour. A few years ago, U. S. Army engineers, using a scientific device, timed some of Bob Feller's fast ones. They found the ball traveled 146 feet a second—98.6 miles an hour.

That means a batter has just two-fifths of a second to decide whether the ball that has just left the pitcher's hand is one that he believes he can hit or whether to let it go by as a bad one.

When the batter stands at the plate he must stand within a space 6 feet long and 4 feet wide known as the "batter's box." One of these boxes is to the right of the plate for left-handed hitters, the other to the left for right-handers.

To hit the ball, or to make the try, the batter is equipped with the most important item in the game next to the ball itself, the bat. The bat is permitted to be as long as 42 inches, but most of baseball's leading batters do not use bats longer than 35 inches. In a bat of that length there is an area of about seven inches by the two-and-three-quarter-inch thickness that is the effective zone. That's where the ball should be hit squarely to receive the greatest impetus.

A good batter knows that there is much more to batting than just taking a terrific swipe at the ball to see how far you can knock it. Batting is one phase of baseball where form counts. You can't fake being a good batter; either you are or you aren't. Of course, there are some occasions when you may be lucky, but even those are few and far between and no batter in the big leagues depends on luck.

If you will add up the four elements required of a naturally good batter, you will find that they can be expressed in the phrase: "good timing." It goes without saying that it takes strong muscles in the arms, shoulders and wrists to be a top-flight hitter. Quick judgment is also required; how quickly a batter has to think you can find out for yourself if you take a stop watch and measure the

[THE BATTER]

time interval represented by two-fifths of a second. That's even less time than it sounds.

Let's go back to the bat for a minute. You should never select a bat just because somebody else uses that model, or because it carries the autograph of a big league star. Bats come in many sizes and weights, some short and some long, some heavy and some light.

It will take some time before you find a bat which you feel is the one for you. When you do, you will discover that you can swing it comfortably but that it is also somewhat heavy. Don't pick a bat that feels too light just because you can swing it more easily. You'll need weight in your bat if you are to get any distance on your hits.

It's comfort that counts in a bat; choose the bat that feels most comfortable, because then you can handle it best. There are two things in a ball game that must always be under control, the ball and the bat. And if your bat is too heavy or too light, or too long or too short, it will not be under control.

Given the bat in your hand you now have to grip it. The best way to hold a bat is to have it in perfect balance. Most batters find that they can achieve perfect balance when they hold the bat with the hands close together, not more than four inches from its smaller end. Some great batsmen, however, Ty Cobb included, used to hold their bats with their hands five or six inches apart. The grip near the end of the bat characterizes the "swing" hitter, which category takes in most of the major league batters.

On the other hand, there is the "choke" hitter, the batter who holds the bat as much as six inches of the way up the shaft and swings with an abbreviated stroke. The choke hitter gets no more than a three-quarter swing at the ball but in his way he may be as effective as the swing hitter at the required moment.

The choke hitter does not usually hit the ball as far as the swing hitter when the latter connects; the choke hit-

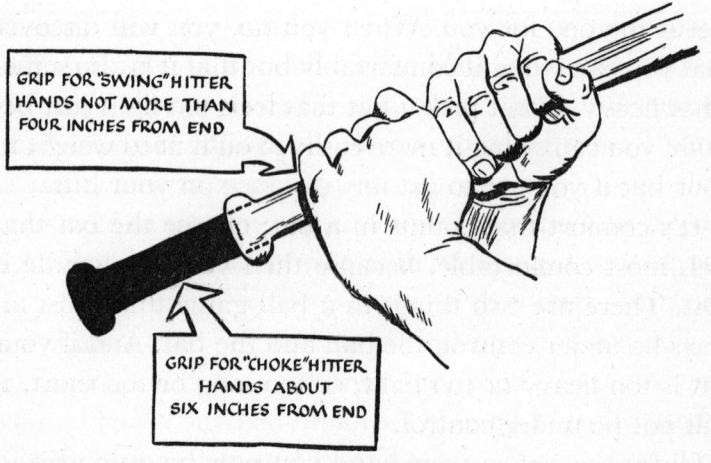

ter, however, connects more often than the swing hitter. But the choke hitter can place his hits much more efficiently than a swing hitter because he has much better control of the bat.

If the strategy of the game demands that a ball be hit to a certain spot at a given moment, a choke hitter will be much more apt to do so than a swing hitter.

Now you're standing in the batter's box waiting for the pitch. The first thing you need is good eyesight. You need good eyesight because you have to watch the ball from

[THE BATTER]

the moment the pitcher starts his windup until you have completed your swing or the ball has landed in the catcher's mitt. You also have to be a good judge of distance so that you will know in advance whether the ball is going to be in the strike zone or whether you should let it go by for a called ball. This judgment of distance calls for good vision.

All great batters have had excellent eyesight. Some league-leaders may have worn eyeglasses to correct faulty vision; Dominic DiMaggio, Bob Dillinger and Paul Waner are notable examples. There is a story about the great Rogers Hornsby, one of the leading hitters in baseball history, that in the twenty years or more that he played in the major leagues, he never went to see a moving picture because he didn't want to subject his eyes to the strain involved.

The position you take in the batter's box is known as the "stance." There are several types of stance. Assuming a batter is right-handed, he might take the "even" stance, with both feet the same distance from the inside line of the batter's box. Or he might take the "closed" stance, with the left foot closer to the inside line. The other stance is the "open" stance, with the right foot closer to the inside line.

The weight should be on the right foot with the knees somewhat relaxed. The batter should take a firm grip on the ground with his spikes. You may stand to the rear of the batter's box or closer to the line nearest the pitcher, but wherever you stand you should be as comfortable as you can. When the ball comes toward you, you should not pull away from the plate.

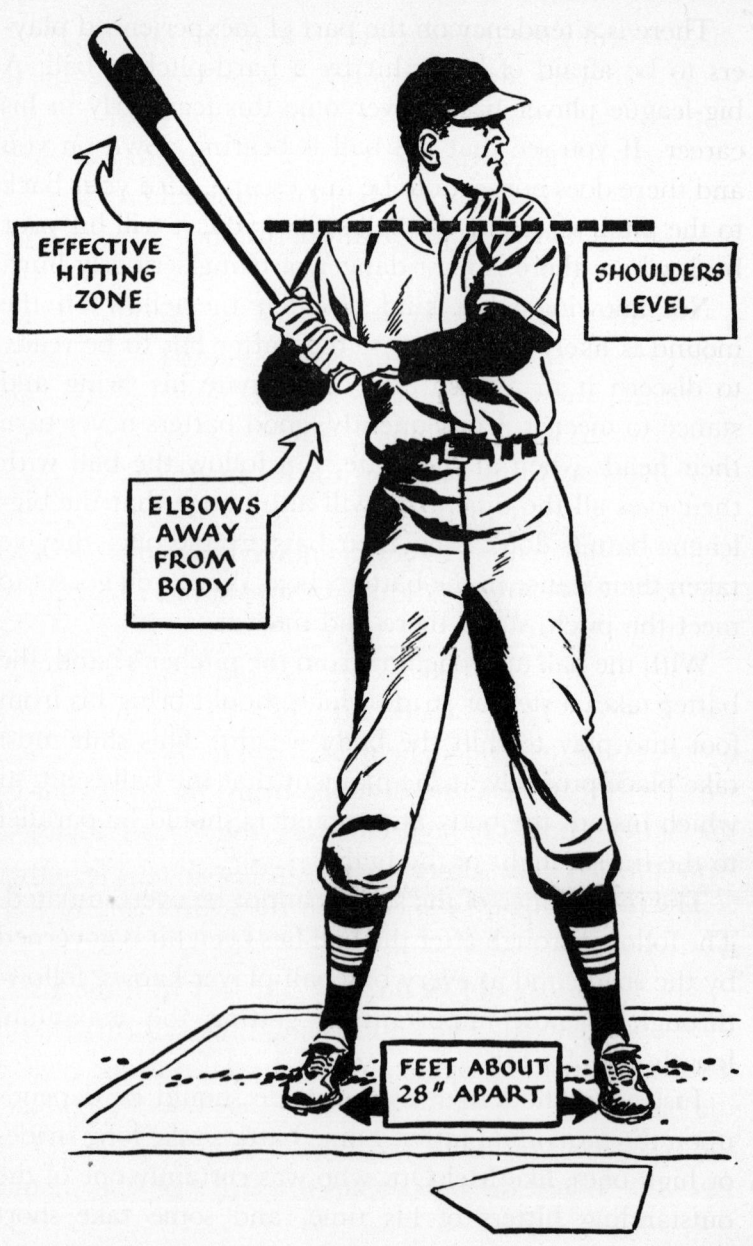

[THE BATTER]

There is a tendency on the part of inexperienced players to be afraid of being hit by a hard-pitched ball. A big-league player has to overcome this fear early in his career. If you see that the ball is bearing down on you and there does not seem to be any escape, turn your back to the pitch so that if the ball strikes you, it will hit your back where there is least danger of being seriously hurt.

Not knowing what kind of pitch the fellow on the mound is likely to send over, the batter has to be ready to discern it in a flash and co-ordinate his swing and stance to meet it. Consequently, good batters never turn their heads when at the plate, but follow the ball with their eyes all the time. You will also notice that the big-league batters don't wave their bats around once they've taken their stance in the batter's box. When you get set to meet the pitch, stand there and meet it.

With the ball approaching from the pitcher's hand, the batter takes a step or stride which should bring his front foot into play to shift the body weight. This shift must take place precisely at the moment that the ball is hit, at which instant the body and shoulders should be parallel to the line of flight of the ball.

The importance of the stride cannot be overestimated. The follow-through after the ball has been hit is governed by the stride and as every baseball player knows, follow-through is most important in getting the maximum length out of a hit.

Just what the length of the stride should be depends upon the individual hitter. Some batters take long strides or high ones, like Mel Ott, who was certainly one of the outstanding hitters of his time, and some take short

[THE BATTER]

strides, like Joe DiMaggio, whose step is less than a foot. The length of the stride and the manner of taking it varies with the batting style and the physique of the batter.

Very few batters in the big leagues raise the striding foot very high; in taking the stride the foot is virtually shuffled forward on the ground.

One of the greatest players ever to play with the Athletics was Al Simmons, a terrific right-handed hitter. They used to call him "Bucket Foot" because he pulled his left foot away from the ball as he swung at it. I noticed this as soon as Al joined the team, and ordinarily I would have suggested that he try to correct it.

But he did so well at batting even in spite of this unorthodox procedure that I never suggested he try to remedy it. That is something I should like to bring up at this point.

There are certain positions and procedures that are considered orthodox in baseball and if a youngster comes up from the minor leagues or the sand lots and doesn't do a thing in the way that tradition has prescribed, a good many managers and coaches will be inclined to make him change to conform. I don't believe in that philosophy.

As in the case of Al Simmons, if a fellow can lead the league in batting with "one foot in the bucket" or even with both feet there, I am inclined to let him alone because that's his natural stance, and a player will always do a thing better if he does it naturally than if some other technique is forced upon him.

That also holds true of the swing. A batter should always try to level off his swing—that is, swing his bat in a line parallel to the ground. A level swing takes advantage of the maximum power, and since your bat is in the same plane with the ball, your chances of meeting the ball are greater. So try for a level swing.

A right-handed batter can guide the swing of the bat by keeping his left elbow in close to the body. If the ball is low in the strike zone, the bat can be lowered, or on the

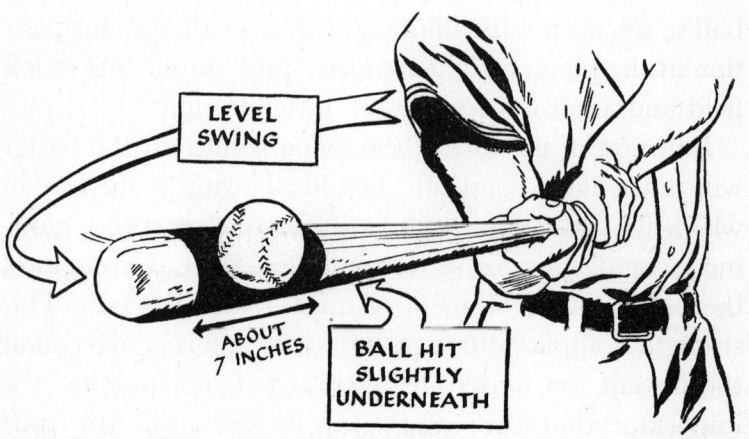

other hand, if the ball is high, the bat can be raised, but no matter whether the swing is high or low in the strike zone, it should be level.

Holding the bat in a comfortable, relaxed attitude, the batter cocks his wrists. As he does so, the bat will move back slightly. It is then swung around the body and held in position as all the muscular strength of the arms, shoulders and wrists is concentrated in anticipation of the pitch.

At the same time as the wrists are cocked, the step or "stride" described above is taken and the weight of the

[THE BATTER]

body is shifted. In the case of a right-handed batter, the step being taken with the left foot, the weight shifts partly to the left leg, which should be held straight with no bend at the knee.

One great fault of young batsmen is that they hurry the swing. If they meet the ball before it reaches the body and if by good fortune they connect solidly, the hit will be what is known as a "pull" hit. A "pull" hitter hits the ball to the part of the diamond corresponding to his position at the plate; a right-handed "pull" hitter hits to left field and a left-handed "pull" hitter to right.

But most of the time if the swing is hurried the batter will not make a solid hit. The ideal swing is the one in which the bat comes round with increasing speed, gaining force all the time so that it carries the top strength of the batter at the moment of impact with the ball. This strength is applied through the wrists and is poured on at the instant the wrists are uncocked. Consequently it is important that the wrists stay cocked until the split second that the bat hits the ball. Ted Williams is an expert at this technique; he has the ability to gauge that elusive instant when the ball and bat meet and to uncock his wrists simultaneously.

If the wrists are uncocked too soon, the power is wasted. After the bat has been applied to the ball, the batter must complete the follow through. In doing so, he continues to swing the bat until the heavy end has come past his other shoulder. This continuous flow of motion and power will add to the length of the distance the ball will travel.

A great deal has been written about the technique of

hitting, and a great deal more remains to be written. It is enough to say, however, that given the natural attributes of a batter, a great hitter can be made by a discerning coach or manager. A change in stance, a shortening or lengthening of the stride, moving in closer to the plate or away from it—all these and many other variations in one's batting position may change a .200 hitter into a .300 ranking batter.

There is one aspect of batting that has to do with strategy: bunting. Inexperienced batters quite often prove ineffective bunters because they try to bunt anything that is pitched to them instead of waiting for the good ones. Then, too, they start to run too quickly—sometimes even before the ball has been hit. That's bad baseball. The batter should wait until the ball has been bunted before taking off for first base.

Bunting calls for lots of practice because it also calls for a much different technique from hitting. The bat is held loosely as the batter takes a natural batting position. The upper hand grips the bat about halfway along its length; the lower hand guides it. The bat must be under perfect control, even though the grip is not as hard as it would be if the batter intended to take a full swing at the ball.

If the bat is held too firmly, the ball will be hit harder, and that is not the aim of the bunt.

A ball that is bunted properly will land on the ground with little or no momentum. The bunt is used mostly as a sacrifice maneuver to advance a runner. However, there have been some fast base runners who have made a specialty of beating out infield bunts. Phil Rizutto, of the

[THE BATTER]

Yankees, is a bunting specialist, but he is also amazingly fast around the bases and it is not uncommon to see him beat out a bunt and land safely on first base.

Left-handed batters find an advantage in the drag

bunt, which is hit just hard enough on the turf between first base and the pitcher's box to be out of reach of the pitcher and yet slow enough to prevent the second baseman from fielding it in time for the putout. The advantage for the southpaw hitter is that he is a step nearer first base than a right-handed batter would be because of his natural position in the batter's box.

Right-handed batters push the ball instead of dragging it; the point at which it should land is between the pitcher and first base, and if the intention of the batter to pull the bunt is well concealed, it is often effective.

With the bat under such close control, the batter can decide whether he wants to place the bunt down the first-base line or the third-base line. A southpaw batter should bunt outside pitches down the third-base line, inside pitches down the first-base line. A right-handed batter does just the reverse. Unless this procedure is followed, the batter will find himself off balance and will be unable to get a quick start for first base, which is essential in beating out a bunt. High balls are difficult to bunt, as there is a tendency for the ball to be popped up.

Young batters should remember not to start running before the ball hits the bat. I know that some of the big-league batters do so, but they have had plenty of experience. Even then a good many of them have to come back because in their haste to get away toward first base they have bunted foul. Best thing is to be sure that the ball has been bunted fair and then head for first.

PITCHING

EVERYONE who knows anything about baseball knows that the pitcher is the most important member of the team.

Major league scouts are always looking for likely material for any position, but most of all for pitchers. As this is written, I have 38 players on my reserve list for next year; of these, 13, or almost one-third, are pitchers. That's how important pitchers are in winning baseball campaigns.

Whether a team wins a baseball game or not depends on its pitcher. He is the defensive anchor. He is the one man on the team who comes into active competition with every member of the opposing side. He carries most of the load—some players put it as high as 75 per cent.

To carry that load there are certain essentials that are absolute "musts" if a player wants to be a star pitcher.

The first, and most important, of these requisites is a *fast ball*. Without speed on the ball, you can't hope to make the major leagues. Having set that down as the Number One requirement, I can go on to tell you what else a big-league pitcher needs.

Next is the matter of *size*. It takes a lot of strength and stamina to pitch a nine-inning game against a major league team. The average pitcher works about every fourth day of a five-month season. As a general rule, pitchers are fairly big fellows; their weight, properly used, gives additional speed to their fast pitches. Height, too, is important because it can help give leverage on a pitch.

But don't get the idea that a little fellow can't be a major league hurler. If a little fellow has everything else that a pitcher needs, including the strength to pitch a full-length game, there's no reason why he can't make the grade. Bobby Shantz, a regular on the Athletics' pitching staff, stands only five feet seven inches tall, but in his last year in the minor leagues, pitching for the Lincoln, Nebraska, club, he won 18 and lost only 7. He struck out 212 men in 214 innings, 14 of them in a single game.

A pitcher need not be able to run fast, or even to hit hard, although both abilities are always welcomed by a manager. Speed of foot is important to a pitcher only from the aspect of fielding, not of base running. Most managers are so tickled to find the other major-league requisites in a pitcher-recruit that they mentally waive the batting and running requirements.

There's one more element that a major-league pitcher needs and that's *courage*. I don't mean the kind of cour-

[PITCHING]

age that it takes to dash into a burning building to rescue someone inside, or to dive through the ice to rescue a drowning person. That calls for heroism, which is something more than courage.

Baseball courage is the thing that makes you stay in there pitching, giving your team all you've got to achieve victory when the tide is running against you, when the breaks are all wrong and when you're on the short end of the score.

A major league pitcher has to have steady nerves. A fellow with the jitters isn't much good when he's pitching to a DiMaggio or a Ted Williams. When the race is close and your team is coming down the home stretch in September, battling either to make or to hold first place, the situation calls for cool, calm, collected confidence in yourself and your fast one.

But of all these things there are two indispensables: A *fast ball* and *control*.

These two items the would-be pitcher must have in advance; the rest of the pitching refinements can be added later through coaching and teaching and practice—that is, if the player is intelligent and watchful and is willing to give it the effort it will take.

Speed without control is not enough. It doesn't matter how fast you can throw the ball if you cannot make it go where you want it to go. It is the combination of the two that enables you to qualify for a berth with the big-league teams.

I am often asked this question: "Can a player develop a fast ball if he doesn't already have it?" I would say: "No."

The fast ball is something a player either has or doesn't have. If he doesn't have it, I don't believe that any amount of practice is going to develop it for him. Quite a number of players have come up to the major leagues in other positions who later became pitchers when their managers discovered they could pitch a fast ball.

So my advice to you is: If you don't have a fast ball, don't try to pitch. Try for some other position on the team.

I will say this: Many a chap will show up at spring practice with a lot of speed on the ball, but he may not know how to get the most out of it. With instruction, such a fellow can smooth out his delivery; by practice and application he can get more of his body into the throw, thus adding to his speed.

Now, about *control:* Have you ever considered the precision marksmanship involved in pitching? Think of this: The pitcher stands 60 feet, 6 inches away from the hitter. The ball, in order to be counted as a strike, has to be thrown through the strike zone. The strike zone is the area measured by the width of the home plate (12 inches at its widest point) and the distance between the armpit and knee of a man averaging about 5 feet 10 inches in height, or about thirty-six inches.

It isn't generally thought about, but the actual strike zone may vary with each player. If his natural batting position is a crouch, for instance, the height of the strike zone decreases. It's contrary to the rules for a player to change his position with each ball pitched; if he does, the umpire may call a strike if a passed ball would have been inside the particular player's strike zone.

So the pitcher has first to concentrate on getting his fast ball across the plate between the batter's armpit and knees. After he has learned to do this consistently, he can go on to other developments, but the basic things come first.

One basic thing in pitching is the stance. Correct stance is something a would-be pitcher should learn at the outset. Under the rules of major-league baseball, the pitch must be made from a "rubber," actually the "pitching plate," which is twenty-four inches long and six inches wide. On the pitch, one foot has to be in contact with the rubber.

Now let's go through a pitch from start to finish. Let's assume you are pitching and you are a right-hander. There is nobody on base, and in order to deceive the batter, you are going to take a full wind-up. You stand behind the rubber until you get the signal from the catcher. A fast one, right across the middle, he signals. All right, let's go!

First comes the *wind-up*. In the old days of baseball, pitchers went through the most complicated acrobatics and gyrations because they thought they could confuse the hitters. But the best pitchers soon discovered that they could conserve their needed energy for the pitch itself by cutting out the twisting wind-up.

Raise the arms over and back of the head with the hands together. The glove should be held in such a way that the batter cannot see the grip you have on the ball. This "stretch," as it is called, will loosen the muscles of the arm and back. You will put a lot more on the ball if

[PITCHING]

you can put the added weight of your body behind the pitch.

Besides, it is much more exhausting to pitch with the arm alone than it is to use the entire series of back muscles.

From the "stretch" position, you begin to pivot rightward on the right foot. As you do so, you should either kick high with the left leg and knee, or, if you find it easier, take a long stride with the left leg. At the same time, turn your body away from the batter.

This should leave you balancing yourself on the right foot, with your right arm back and your left leg forward. Now bring your right arm forward for the pitch.

Continue with the *follow-through* by bringing the right foot forward. Don't bring it close to the body, but in somewhat of an arc, place the right foot even with the left. The effort of the throw should leave your body in something of a crouch, but poised on the front part of your feet, ready to go after the ball if it is batted back into the vicinity of the pitching mound.

Once you've started your pitching motion, you may not stop without being guilty of a balk. You may not throw to a base without taking a step in the direction of that base; it is a balk if, with your foot on the rubber, you make a move to throw to a base and do not do so. Finally, when holding a man on base, you must come to a pause as you join your hands together in front of you before speeding the ball to the catcher. Otherwise you are guilty of a balk which advances all base-runners one base.

Many pitchers waste a good deal of energy during a

game by taking a few steps toward the plate after every pitch. That's not sound baseball. The pitcher needs every ounce of strength he possesses, and he shouldn't use it up walking around the diamond. I always tell my pitchers to

1. FORWARD STANCE FOR WINDUP RIGHT FOOT ON RUBBER

2. SIDEWARD STANCE WITH MEN ON BASE — NO WINDUP — RIGHT FOOT ALONG EDGE OF RUBBER

hold their positions until they get the ball back from the catcher. The pitcher then can return behind the rubber and with one step he's in pitching position again.

When it comes to pitching the ball in actual play, there are three questions to be decided:

How are you going to throw it?

What kind of pitch are you going to throw?

[PITCHING]

Where are you going to throw it?

There are three ways to throw a baseball: Over-arm, side-arm and under-arm. Under-arm delivery need not be discussed. It is so difficult to master that it is very little used. However, in passing, if an underhand fast ball is given a forward spin, it makes one of the most effective drop-balls in use.

The most-used style of pitching is the over-arm delivery. It is the easiest to master and it is the most natural way to throw a baseball. The over-arm throw will give a fast ball a "hop," and it will cause a curve ball to "hook" or "drop."

A tall pitcher has the advantage over a hitter when he pitches with the over-arm delivery. From the elevation of the pitching mound the ball comes down across the plate at an angle so that the batter has difficulty facing it squarely.

There are two variations of the over-arm delivery, the full delivery and the three-quarter. In the full delivery, the arm passes directly over the shoulder in a full vertical arc; in the three-quarter, the arm comes forward about three-quarters of the way between vertical and horizontal.

More difficult to master, but with some advantages when pitching a curve ball, is the side-arm delivery. Here the arm swings forward parallel to the ground. The pitching arc is horizontal instead of vertical as in the over-arm delivery. Pitch a fast ball with the side-arm delivery and it will "hop" in toward the batter; if he hits it at all, it will most likely be a weak pop-up or a slow grounder.

Now as I said at the outset of this chapter, a major league pitcher has to have a fast ball. Having a fast ball, he can develop a curve with enough practice. After he gets the curve ball down pat, he can also develop a slow ball, usually referred to as a "change of pace."

There are also a few types of throws that have been developed by individual pitchers: Christy Mathewson's "fadeaway," and Carl Hubbell's terrific "screwball," which was the bane of all opposing batters. But these were unusual; the principal equipment of a pitcher is a fast ball, a curve and a "change of pace." Let's discuss each one.

To throw a *fast ball* effectively, it should be held between the thumb and the first and second fingers. The thumb will be underneath, the fingers above. The third finger and little finger lie folded against the palm. The first and second fingers should be extended along the seams, where the raised stitches will help to control the

[PITCHING]

ball and give it spin. Hold the ball in the fingertips, not in the palm of the hand. Don't hold it tightly.

Using the over-arm delivery, when the fast ball leaves the pitcher's hand, the fingers should be on top of the ball. It is thus given a backward spin which will make it

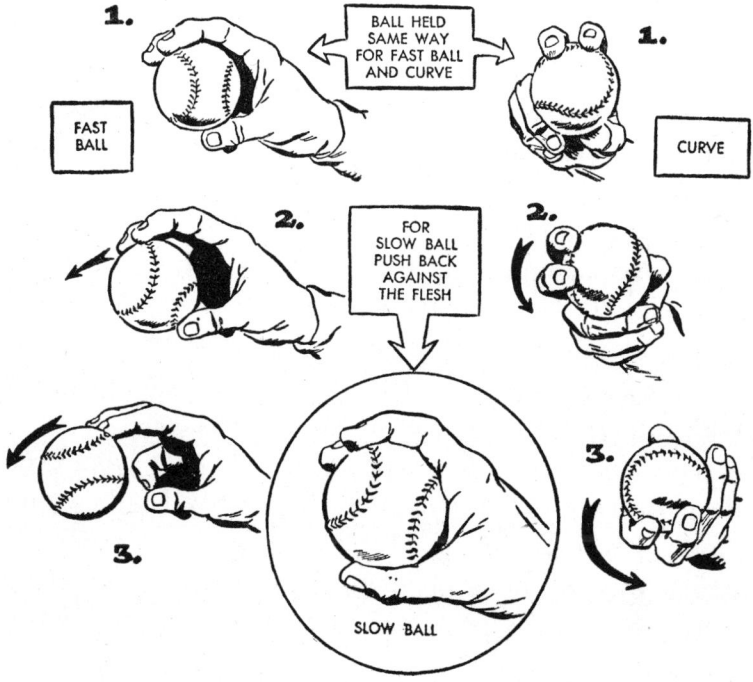

rise or "hop" as it nears the plate. Be careful not to let the ball leave the fingers too soon; if the swing of the arm is not a full one, the pitch will be too high.

For a good fast ball, the pitcher doesn't twist his fingers or his wrist.

Now for the *curve ball*. The ball is held the same as for

a fast ball, but as it leaves the hand, there should be a sharp outward snap of the wrist. The ball should leave the hand along the line of the index finger, between that finger and the thumb. The fingers and thumb will be at the sides of the ball, not top and bottom as in the fast ball.

Give the wrist a full snap. When the pitch is completed, the arm must be all the way back and the pitcher's shoulder will point toward the batter.

A right-handed pitcher will spin his curve ball toward the outside of the plate, away from a right-handed batter. A left-handed pitcher's curve travels in just the opposite fashion. Since it's harder to hit a curve ball breaking away from a batter, managers generally send a left-handed pinch hitter in against a right-handed pitcher and vice versa.

The *slow ball* is the major league pitcher's strategy ball. It may be thrown as a straight ball or a curve but it's slow. It is generally thrown when the pitcher has been tossing fast ones and curves and he has reason to believe the batter will be expecting more of the same. If worked correctly, it will lead the batter to swing too soon and may also make him swing too late on the following fast one.

In execution, the slow ball is just like the other two pitches I have described. It is thrown with the same motion, but the tips of the fingers are raised slightly, or the pressure is lessened as the ball is tossed. You give the slow ball no finger snap and a minimum of wrist action, consequently the speed of the ball is cut down.

Of course, a smart pitcher will not throw a slow ball across the heart of the plate. If he does, a middling good batter may slam it out of the park. So be careful when you

[PITCHING]

throw the change of pace ball not to place it too conveniently near the hitter's bat.

In order to be a successful major league pitcher, not only do you have to know a lot about pitching, but you have to know a great deal about hitting, even if you are not a .320 hitter yourself.

As I said before, your objective is to make the batter strike out but you can do this in two ways. You can overpower him with superior pitching, or you can pitch to his weakness and make him help you beat him.

Have you ever watched players sitting on the bench during a game or even during batting practice? Have you noticed how intent they are in watching their opponents in action? I make it one of the cardinal rules of the game to know everything possible about the weaknesses and the strength of the individual players on teams opposing the Athletics.

You can take it for granted that every pitcher in the American League knows what kind of pitch to avoid when facing Ted Williams or Joe DiMaggio. That's because these two leaders have been studied by every pitcher who has to pitch to them.

To know where to pitch to a batter, you must first study his position. If he stands away from the plate, pitch him one on the outside that he may be tempted to go for. If he can't reach it and moves in closer awaiting the next pitch, let him have one inside.

If you have a batter who stands close to the plate, keep trying to pitch inside to him.

Also, watch the batter's stride. If he takes too long a stride and is thus too far forward, pitch high and inside to him. A change of pace ball will generally find a player of this type off balance, too.

Pay close attention to the batter's individual mannerisms. You will find that virtually every player has some nervous mannerisms at the plate. If they occur during the flight of the ball, they can destroy his timing and make his batting ineffective.

Of course, in precision pitching, such as big league pitching must be, you must have a target. A pitcher can't just throw his fast ball and hope for the best. I think a young pitcher will find it well to do what my old battery mate of sixty years ago used to do—Jim Whitney was his name. I was then a catcher.

He used to pick some particular spot on my uniform and aim for that. If the batter liked a high ball, he would pitch for my knee; if the hitter couldn't pound out the high ones, Jim would aim for my shoulders. For one who was weak on inside balls, the mark was my corresponding shoulder, and vice versa for a hitter who didn't like them outside.

The main idea is to outguess and outmaneuver the batter. Concentrate on the fast ball but don't forget to throw in a slow one now and then. For most hitters, the high ones inside will stop them. The curve should be used when there are two strikes against the batter.

Don't throw a slow ball to a weak hitter. Above all, never underestimate the man facing you at the plate. You must pitch to every opponent as though he were leading the league in batting averages, even though he's near the bottom of the list. I repeat, don't underestimate any batter, even a pitcher.

[PITCHING]

I've known many pitchers who were inclined to let down for the moment when the opposing pitcher came to bat. That's bad baseball. A pitcher like Lou Brissie can break up a game with a home run if his opposing moundsman lets down when Lou is at bat.

Lastly, the pitcher should be calm and reserved at all times, no matter what is going on on the diamond. At times there will be arguments with the umpire. After all, let's face it—players are sometimes tempted to dispute an arbiter's decision.

But such disputes are not the province of the pitcher. The catcher, coaches, captain or manager can do the arguing if there is any to be done. But if you let yourself get upset over an umpire's decision, the chances are that your effectiveness for that particular game is over. So take a tip from an old-timer: Take it easy!

THE CATCHER

THE CATCHER plays more actual baseball than any other member of the team. The man behind the plate is generally the fellow who calls the play. He is the one player who faces his own entire team and can convey information to his team-mates. A smart catcher, one who is full of pep, can make a mediocre team good and a good team excellent.

I have always had a soft spot in my heart for the catching position for it was as a catcher that I broke into baseball. As a young fellow I stood six feet four and a half inches, and I found in playing baseball on my home town team at East Brookfield, Massachusetts, that my height stood me in good stead.

From behind the plate I could survey the playing field and give instructions to the other members of my team. I was as thin in those days as I am now; my top weight

[THE CATCHER]

in the National League some years later was about 150 pounds.

I was the only one who wore a glove. The other players snickered at the idea of wearing gloves to play baseball. In those days the pitcher stood forty feet from the plate and the catcher about twelve feet behind it. The ball was usually caught behind the plate on its first bounce. Generally the ball was thrown underhand, and a batter could, if he wished, call for the pitcher to throw a high or a low one.

So that I could buy a buckskin glove, the fellows on the team each contributed a dime. I clipped the fingertips off the glove and sewed the remaining ends together—this was my first catcher's "mitt."

One pleasant experience I had as a catcher I will remember all my life—the time in 1884 when I caught against Yale's baseball team. It was the day I was being given a tryout with the Meriden, Connecticut, club and our opponent was the Yale freshman team. Yale's team was very powerful and in order to get competition worthy of its mettle, the Blue often would schedule a game or two with a professional ball club. Pitching for Yale that day was Amos Alonzo Stagg, who could play baseball as well as he could play football.

We met again on the baseball diamond in 1888 when Yale played an exhibition game with the Washington Senators—Stagg pitched for the Bulldogs and I caught for Washington.

In a way I had something to do with the development of the catcher's mitt in those days. When I played for Hartford in the South New England League in 1885, one of my teammates, Bill Gray, suggested I try out a rubber catching pad he had invented. Another catcher and myself were the first to wear the pads; the other fellow said it would never do, but I found it very helpful.

Gray sold his patent to Spalding's for $5000; from this patent developed the modern catcher's mitt. Meanwhile, I had discovered that I could take a good bit of the sting out of the fast ones if I put a slice of steak into my palm when I put on my thin makeshift glove. A good many catchers adopted this device after it became generally known.

Times haven't changed much since then so far as catchers are concerned; catchers of major-league caliber are still hard to come by. Day after day in the baseball season scouts beat the bushes roundly in an effort to find catchers for the major-league teams. Let me tell you what they look for in a catcher:

First, physique. A good catcher obviously needs certain physical requirements. I don't believe it matters whether he be tall or short, but he should be well built and rugged. Most big league catchers are fairly large-sized, but that doesn't bar a slim, wiry fellow from the job if he can take it.

A catcher MUST have a good, strong throwing arm and fairly large hands. He must be able to catch every one of the pitcher's deliveries, which calls not only for strength but endurance, too, because next to the pitcher, the greatest strain of a baseball game falls on the catcher. His body, arms and feet must have good co-ordination so that he can throw to any base without wasting a fraction of a second. Most major-league batsmen are such

[THE CATCHER]

good runners that a half-second can sometimes be the difference between an out and a run scored.

A catcher must not only catch, but hold the ball, and that's where a big pair of hands come into consideration in choosing a major-league catcher. In the course of a season a catcher may handle as many as 10,000 pitched balls; on the average, only about a dozen of these get away from a first-class catcher.

There was one ball that got away from a catcher that cost a World Series. In the fourth game of the 1941 Series between the Brooklyn Dodgers and the New York Yankees, Tommy Henrich of the Yankees was at bat in the ninth inning with two men out. The Yankees had won two games, Brooklyn one. With two strikes against him, Tommy swung and missed.

So did Mickey Owen, the Dodgers' catcher, and a great baseball player. The ball got away from him, and Henrich dashed for first base. Although Brooklyn led at that point, 4 to 3, the Yankees staged one of those great rallies for which they have been famous, and went on to win, 7 to 4. They followed with another victory and won the Series.

Besides being physically on his toes throughout the game, the catcher has to be mentally on his toes, too. The element that makes a catcher really great is his shrewdness and fast thinking behind the plate. It is the catcher who signals for the type of pitch he thinks should be tossed to the batter—like the quarterback on the football gridiron, he calls the play.

Consequently, a big-league catcher constantly studies the opposing batsmen, learning their styles of hitting, their positions and swing and any other personal habits, always looking for the opponent's strength or weakness.

I might point out that many of baseball's smartest players have been the fellows behind the plate—men like Mickey Cochrane, Bill Dickey, Ossie Schreck and Johnny Kling, for example.

The catcher has moved up closer to the batter since the days when I was the man behind the plate. Of course, he has more protection today against injury than we had in the old days. Despite that, however, the catcher is more open to injury than any other player when the game is being played for keeps.

There are some simple rules about the catching position which if followed will reduce the probability of injury. Every big-league catcher knows them and if you watch the catcher closely the next time you go to a ball game you will see how he puts them into practice. I will give them to you here as we go along.

To give his signals, the catcher takes his position behind the plate. His feet should be only a few inches apart, pointing straight ahead. He squats with the weight of his body on the balls of his feet. The trunk of the body should be bent slightly forward.

The left arm should rest on the left thigh; the gloved hand should extend beyond the knee, with the palm turned inward. The signals are given with the fingers of the right hand, which should be below the flap of the catcher's chest protector.

In this way, the signals are hidden from the first-base coaching line and from a possible runner on first. The mitt hides the signals from the coach on the third-base

[THE CATCHER]

line and can also be used to conceal the signals from a possible runner on second base who could, by his own signal, relay information to the batter or the opposing bench.

After giving the signals the catcher assumes a more straightened position behind the plate. The stance should

straddle home plate, with the feet about 20 inches apart, but not too far apart to prevent the catcher from shifting quickly to either side if the ball is wide.

The weight should be kept slightly forward on the balls of the feet. Most big league catchers place the left foot five or six inches ahead of the right to enable them to throw to any of the bases without extra footwork. The ball should never be received while the catcher is squatting on his heels because he is then out of position for foul and bunted balls as well as high or wide ones.

The position of the catcher on receiving pitches is very important because the pitcher uses the catcher's body as his target. Thus, for low inside and outside pitches, the pitcher sights along the catcher's knees; for high inside or outside throws the catcher's shoulders serve as the target points. The mitt and the bare hand, which ballplayers sometimes call the "meat hand," also help the catcher show the pitcher where he wants the ball thrown.

Now a hard-thrown ball has a lot of force behind it and unless you learn to catch it properly you are apt to get some hurt fingers. So a major-league catcher always takes all pitches below the waist with his fingers pointing downward; all above-the-waist throws are caught with the fingers pointing upward. Not only is this method safer for the fingers but it also enables the catcher to handle the ball more quickly.

As soon as the ball is caught in the mitt, preferably in the pocket, the other hand should be clapped over the ball. At the same time, the mitt hand should give a little to lessen the force of the impact. The bare hand should, until the ball strikes the mitt, remain in a relaxed clinch; to keep it open is inviting injury from the pitched ball. At the same moment as the ball strikes the glove, the catcher should open his right hand, grasp the ball and immediately bring it to a throwing position behind his ear with his right arm cocked for a toss to any of the three bases or back to the pitcher.

When I said at the beginning of this chapter that a catcher has to have a good throwing arm and facile

[THE CATCHER]

hands, I should also have mentioned the feet, for footwork is one of the most important factors behind the plate. A good catcher has to be as agile on his feet as a ballet dancer.

Virtually every pitched ball calls for a shift in position. On a ball pitched to his right, the catcher steps over with

his right foot so that his body is in front of the oncoming ball. As the ball lodges in his mitt, the right foot is placed behind and the left foot is moved forward into a balanced position for throwing. When the ball is thrown to the catcher's left, he slides his left foot to the left, as his right foot follows to the rear.

I cannot overestimate the importance of being able to shift the feet without any loss of movement. As I have said before, a split second may be the difference between victory and defeat and the catcher must be in position to throw in time to beat any base runners.

In the case of a bad throw or a wild pitch the catcher cannot hesitate; he must dive or even throw himself in front of the ball and block it with his body, if there are runners on base.

A big-league catcher has to be an expert ball-thrower. His throwing arm is one of his greatest possessions. One thing a catcher must always remember: Get the ball away quickly! Now that doesn't mean that you shouldn't stop to think about what you're doing and where you're throwing the ball. Time should be taken to be accurate; a catcher can lose a game with a wild pitch just as easily as a pitcher can.

Most catchers in the big leagues use the overhand throw but only from the shoulder and not with the full arm sweep. This motion gives the greatest amount of control over the ball and makes it easier to handle. Occasionally a snap throw can be made to first base with a left-hand hitter at the plate, or to third base when a right-hander is up, so as to avoid hitting the batter with the throw. There are other occasions when an underhand throw can be used, as in cases of a run-down between third base and home plate, but for general use, the overhand throw will do.

Under all circumstances the throw should be made with a proper shift of the feet. The throw must be timed perfectly with the shift and the co-ordinated movement of the body. The wrist should not be held too rigid, and the stride with the throw should not be too long.

Among the other duties of the catcher is to field foul

[THE CATCHER]

flies. The first thing the catcher does in going after a foul fly is to discard his mask, so that he will have full vision. The quickest way to get rid of the mask is to flick it off by an upward stroke of the right thumb under the chin guard of the mask. You should be sure, however, to throw it as far as you can when discarding it, so that you will not trip over the mask in going after the ball.

When chasing a foul ball, the body should be turned in the direction from which the pitch was tossed to the batter. If it came in on the left-hand side, it will be fouled off to the left and the catcher should turn to the left. If it came in on the right-hand side, the foul will be on the right, too.

Since the ball is presumably in the air, it will be necessary to turn the head upward to locate it, but once having got the location, the catcher should get directly underneath and then back up a foot or two so that the catch can be made in front of him.

Practically the same procedure is followed in going after pop flies which do not go near enough to first base or third base for the infielders to handle. In catching these flies, the hands should be held close in to the body; if they are held out too far, the ball may be dropped. If the catcher sees that he cannot get the ball, he should call to other members of the team to take it.

Another job the catcher has is to field all bunts that he can get his hands on. This takes speed and determination. He has to take off his mask, as in the case of foul pops and pop flies, and should go after the ball from the left so that he will be in position for the throw when the ball is recovered.

On a bunt play, the catcher should never turn his back to the field. If the bunt is toward third base, the ball should be played from the third-base side of the ball with the catcher facing first or second base, as the play may require. The mitt comes in handy on a bunt play, being used to propel the ball into the throwing hand.

The catcher also has to back up first base if the bases are not occupied where the fielding of a batted ball could result in an over-throw landing between first base and home plate. In such cases the pitcher or third baseman will run in to cover the plate.

It's when the chips are down and a runner is trying to come home from third base on a close play that a catcher proves his mettle. First, he has to have the intestinal fortitude to face the oncoming runner. If you have the ball in your possession you may legally stand there

[THE CATCHER]

and block him; he has the privilege of sliding with his spikes ahead of him, too.

Sometimes the throw will be wide, throwing you off balance or away from the plate. In that case you have to dive for the runner, trying to tag him before he touches the rubber.

Best plan is for the catcher to take a stance on the base line toward third base. The right foot should be a little distance from the plate but blocking the front of the rubber. The left foot should be on the line ahead of the right foot. In this way the runner is forced to go around the catcher to get to the plate. On plays like this, a catcher must remember to get possession of the ball first, then to get the runner out. Sometimes an overzealous catcher will play the runner instead of the ball and lose both.

You must not block the plate, however, unless you have the ball.

The catcher is the nerve-center of the team. He has to direct the action at the plate and in most cases the action on the field. When he signals the pitcher for a particular throw, he must make sure that the other players on the team know what is coming so that they will be ready for any action that has to follow. On bunts, he must call out instructions to the infielders and the pitcher. In general he has to direct the team's defensive strategy. So you can readily see that the catcher carries a very heavy load of responsibility in a ball game.

It is the catcher who tells the pitcher what to throw to a particular batter. Consequently, he has to study every opposing player. When the batter is too close to the plate, the catcher calls for an inside pitch; when the batter is too far from the rubber, the catcher tells the pitcher by his signals to send one outside.

No individual weakness or personal idiosyncrasy is overlooked by a smart catcher when he appraises an opposing batsman. And everything he sees he must convey by means of signals to his team-mates.

Big-league catchers have signals arranged not only with their pitchers but with their infielders, too. The catcher will often try to pick a runner off when he gets the signal from an infielder that it would be worth a try. So there is a regular code of signals, all worked with the fingers.

It is important to prevent the opposing team from finding out what each signal means; a complicated system is generally worked out under which the catcher gives three signs in rapid succession but only the pitcher or the particular infielder knows which is the one intended by the catcher.

A few catchers use the hands in various positions on the body or the glove or the mask to give signals, but the majority convey their signals by means of the fingers. In any case, the signs should be clear and visible to the pitcher, shortstop and second baseman. The latter two players can relay the signals to the other infielders.

Last, but not least in importance, is the part that the catcher plays in helping the pitcher keep his control. The catcher sets the pace for the pitcher. If the latter tries to pitch too hurriedly, the catcher slows him down by calling for time out and walking out to the mound. A pitcher

[THE CATCHER]

who takes his time will have better control than one who, under pressure, has a tendency to throw in a hurry.

The first consideration in winning a ball game is to get the batter out. Consequently, the catcher must do everything he can to help the pitcher; this includes bolstering his morale whenever it becomes necessary. He has to know just how to handle the pitcher and for the sake of the team should praise and encourage the hurler no matter what his feelings may be.

If the catcher is well-liked by all the players on the team, you will probably have a harmonious and victorious ball club; if he is disliked, the manager will soon find himself having to shake things up.

FIRST and THIRD BASE

SOME of the most famous baseball players of all time have been major league first basemen. In the list you will find fellows like Lou Gehrig, Jimmy Foxx, Hank Greenberg, Johnny Mize and Bill Terry.

If you will think about these great players for a moment you will remember that they all have certain qualities in common. First, they are all big, tall and powerful, and mighty men with the bat; second, most of them are left-handed; third, despite their size they were all extremely graceful and fast on their feet. These are the main qualifications that a young fellow needs to make a great first baseman.

In the early days of the major leagues the emphatic

[FIRST AND THIRD BASE]

requirements for a first baseman were size and power at the bat. Today, in addition to those two qualifications, a first baseman has to be almost perfect at catching a ball no matter how it is thrown or hit in his direction.

Now the requirement of size should not rule out a player of medium height provided he has the other requirements, but a fellow with a long body, long legs and long arms who can stretch to receive a ball and still keep his foot on base will have the advantage.

Also very important is the ability in a first baseman to think quickly. He is in a position where his judgment counts for a great deal; it was the ability to think quickly that made Hank Greenberg and Lou Gehrig great players as much as their ability to hit a long ball when a distance clout was required.

It is possible for a right-hander to star at first base, but the southpaw will have the edge because when he throws to second or third base he is in a position to make the throw more quickly than the right-hander, who has to shift. As you can see, however, the right-hander has the advantage on throws to home, but that play occurs infrequently.

The first baseman must have big hands, flexible wrists and strong arms. When he throws to catch a runner at second, third or home the throw must be fast. In fielding he must be able to handle the ball without an instant's hesitation and he must have courage as well because most of his playing is done with a runner bearing down upon him at high speed in an effort to make the base safely. Whenever he can, a good first baseman uses both hands in catching the ball. All major league first basemen are of course adept at the one-handed catch as well. This is obvious since a first baseman can reach farther for a ball with one arm than he can with both.

The play at first base is very often determined by the breadth of a whisker and very often, sitting in the stands, you will say to yourself that an umpire has called a man safe at first when he should have been called out. That is why the first-base umpire has to be very sharp-eyed, and many an argument has resulted from the umpire's decision at first base.

Size is important to a first baseman because of the stretch. In the stress of a game the first baseman is likely to receive a poorly-thrown ball. As he has to keep one foot on the bag, the fellow with a long stretch can offer a bigger target to the other infielders than the first baseman who does not have such a long reach and has to catch the ball within a smaller area.

No ballet dancer ever had to be quicker or more graceful on her feet than a major league first baseman. I have seen slow-motion moving pictures of close plays at first base where the baseman had to go up in the air to retrieve a bad throw, and the action was really beautiful to behold.

The standard position of the first baseman as the ball is pitched is about 15 feet in from the base line and from 15 to 20 feet toward the outfield. However, the first baseman usually changes this position upon instructions from the bench, depending on the speed of the batter and depending also on his own individual agility and speed of foot. As soon as the ball has been hit, the first baseman follows it with his eyes, at the same time taking a position

[FIRST AND THIRD BASE]

in front of his base, facing the infielder who has fielded the ball and is moving to throw it to first base. His stance should be a natural one and the heels should be touching the front of the base. In this position the first baseman can shift to receive the ball from any direction whence it may be thrown. If he has to stretch, the direction of the ball determines which foot is kept in contact with

TOE ONLY TOUCHING THE BAG FOR THE GREATEST STRETCH

the bag. For instance, if the throw is to the right, he stretches with his right foot and tags with his left. No top-flight first baseman will stand on the base awaiting a throw. If he does, he is likely to get knocked over.

Some players have acrobatic ability which they bring into play in covering first base. This is particularly true on the stretch. Where the throw is to the right of first base the first baseman shifts to the right and touches the base with his left toe. The right foot will then be stretched toward the right field. If the throw is to the left of first base, the ball is fielded with the right foot touching the inside corner, the left leg then being extended in the direction of the pitcher or the catcher.

The first baseman has to be able to judge exactly how far he can stretch for a throw, and if he cannot catch the ball retaining contact with the base he may have to leave the base to prevent the ball from getting away. On such occasions, however, the pitcher will run over to cover the base. On this play the first baseman *must* be accurate in his throw.

One rule that every first baseman has to remember is to play the ball rather than the base. The inexperienced player sometimes finds it hard to take his foot off the base in going after a ball when two or three feet more would have meant a recovery and an out. If you will watch a really great first baseman you will see that he does not remain anchored to the base. He goes after the ball wherever it may be and depends upon his speed to get back before the runner gets there.

The first baseman has to shift on virtually every ball thrown or hit. His fielding skill must be on a par at least with that of the other infielders. Consequently, the same rules that apply to fielding generally apply to a first baseman. The first baseman usually goes after ground balls which are hit to his right provided they are hit hard; if the ball is not hit with much force, however, the second baseman will field it and throw to first.

Another reason why the left-handed first baseman has the advantage over the right-hander in throwing to sec-

[FIRST AND THIRD BASE]

ond or third is that he can make the throw, after he has practiced it sufficiently, without even straightening up. Usually the fielding of a ball, the stride in the direction of the base to which he wants to throw and the throw

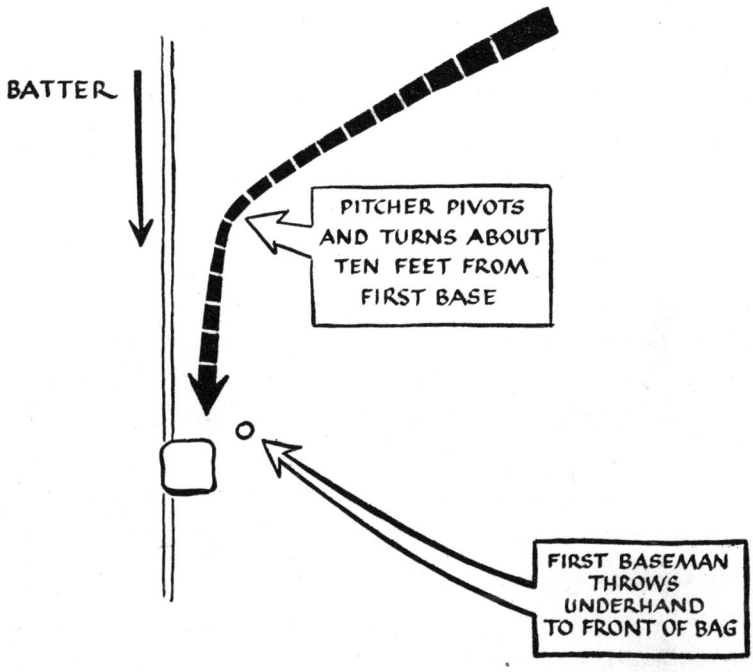

itself seem to be merely one continuous movement whereas for a right-handed first baseman this would involve a complete change of stance during which time the runner might gain the crucial step or two.

The first baseman receives assistance from the pitcher whenever a ball is hit between the pitcher and first base. If the ball is hit to the first baseman the pitcher should run over to cover first. However, he does not run in a direct line to first base. He should slant toward the first base path until he is about 10 feet away from first base and then pivot so that when he arrives at the bag he will be headed in the same direction as the batter. If a first baseman has fielded the ball and cannot make the play himself, he throws the ball to the pitcher underhand in such a way that the pitcher can take it about chest height a few feet before he reaches the base.

Another province in which the first baseman must shine is in fielding bunts along a first base line. Here again the ball must be watched closely and if it appears that the batter is going to bunt, the first baseman must come in fast to field the ball. In such cases either the pitcher or the second baseman will run over to cover the bag, depending on whether or not the pitcher is required to field the bunt. In any event, the player retricving the ball should let the others know that he has it and throw to the player covering first base.

More double plays are terminated at first base than at any other point in the diamond and if you were to analyze the double plays made in the course of a season you would find that fewer of them are throws from first to second and back again than any other combination of tosses. His ability to make this difficult play more easily is one reason why a left-handed first baseman has an advantage over a right-hander. Having fielded a ball, he can throw to second base without pivoting and can then run back to first to receive the throw from second.

Now a right-handed first baseman has to be more careful on his initial throw to second. He will generally throw it overhand and he will also have to pivot to make the

[FIRST AND THIRD BASE]

throw. The right-hander can make double plays but not so easily as the left-hander.

Of course the first baseman also has to take all pop flies in his area. Sometimes a second baseman will call for a pop fly behind first base, as his angle of approach to the ball makes it an easier catch for him than for the first baseman.

The general impression is that a third baseman has it easier, but this is not a fact. Third base can be a very hot corner and a good third baseman can sometimes be the most valuable player of the team. As a matter of fact, in 1947 Bob Elliott of the Boston Braves was chosen as the most valuable player in the National League.

A great many major-league third basemen have switched to third base after having played at some other spot in the infield. The third baseman does not have to be as fast as the first baseman because in the course of the ordinary ball game he does not get as many fielding chances. Consequently, a third baseman is chosen with an eye on his batting ability. While a strong arm is of value to a third baseman it is not as much a requisite in the first baseman. The longest throw a third baseman is required to make at any time is to first base, but generally he has ample time in which to make the throw; therefore, the third baseman with a poor throwing arm can compensate for this with the ability to hit a long ball when at bat.

However, the one thing a third baseman *must* be able to do is to handle a bunt. He always has to be ready for it and always has to be in the right position. Because of this, the area that he can cover around third base is limited. Some third basemen like Joe Dugan and Pie Traynor of the Pittsburgh Pirates had almost a sixth sense that told them when the batter intended to bunt.

Sometimes what looks like a bunt is actually a ball at which the batter has taken a full swing but, having been

topped, the ball does not go beyond the infield. It is likely that such an occasion will find the third baseman playing deep and he therefore has to come in fast to recover the ball. The way to handle this kind of hit is to take the ball with the bare hand, and without straightening up throw to first. This is a play where you can tell whether the third baseman has his eye on the ball, for in order to grab the ball with his bare hand he must not lift his head or take his eye off the rolling grounder. Except for such hits, most of the difficult plays which come to the third baseman are very slow hits or terrific smashes which he

[FIRST AND THIRD BASE]

has to knock down even if he cannot catch them, because a ball hit down the third-base foul line will mean extra bases if it lands in the outfield.

Just as the first and second basemen share the responsibility for catching pop flies, so the third baseman shares the foul territory with the catcher so far as pop-ups into either fair or foul territory are concerned. A third baseman has to have determination to go after foul pops which may land in or near the stands. Many a game has been saved by a third baseman who leaned over the railing of the stands as far as he could to catch a foul. It should be noted that it is not against the rules to hold on to the railing with the other hand when reaching into the stands for a foul.

The third baseman has wide latitude in going after pop-ups and even on flies hit to his far right the third baseman should always try for the catch. It sometimes happens that the sun may be in the eyes of the catcher or he may be unable to locate the ball for some other reason, in which event the third baseman can be helpful. Pop flies behind third are often easier catches for the shortstop, just as those behind first are easier for the second baseman than for the first baseman.

Just as the first baseman must be careful of his foot work in covering the initial sack, the third baseman also has to use skill in this direction. Most big-league third basemen try to tag a runner a step or two before the runner has reached third. This works only if the baseman has the ball sufficiently in advance of the arrival of the runner. In any event, he must try to be in front of the base facing either second or home, depending upon the play. Stealing home is not attempted frequently, but one of the functions of the third baseman is to hold a runner close to his base. This is usually accomplished by the pitch to the catcher.

Along with the fielding ability and batting excellence generally expected of a first-class third baseman he must have the competitive spirit and the inclination toward team play that are the marks of good baseball players. The names of the players listed at the beginning of this chapter are those of men who were great "team" men who had the respect and admiration of their teammates, and who, although they were great stars in their individual right, never played the game as individuals but rather as members of the team.

SECOND BASE and SHORTSTOP

SECOND BASE is a crucial spot on the diamond. Indeed, it is so crucial that in defensive baseball it is guarded by two players, the second baseman and the shortstop. In the big leagues, these positions are played in such close co-operation that they are generally spoken of as the "keystone combination." When second-base strategy is being planned for a particular game, the two positions are treated as a unit.

The shortstop plays at second base so often that on plays at the keystone corner he and the second baseman usually have a secret signal between them to indicate which one of them is to handle the play.

Second base and shortstop are the two positions on the ball team in which a small man can shine because while some positions on the team require a big, hulking physique, this is not true of second base or shortstop.

Usually a big build hampers a player in getting around with the agility and speed needed at the shortstop post, although there are exceptions, like Lou Boudreau of the Cleveland Indians.

On the other hand, little Phil Rizzuto of the New York Yankees is so outstanding despite his comparatively small stature that he was named among the most valuable players in the American League for 1949.

I believe that next to the pitcher and the catcher, the shortstop is the most important man on the team. If he's fast on his feet, fields well and can think quickly in a pinch, and if, in addition to these attributes, he can pole out a hit when it's needed, he can be the difference between a first-division team and one that finishes 'way down the list.

One of the most recent examples of how much a good shortstop means to a team is to be found in the Athletics' experience two years ago. At the beginning of the season it was predicted that the team would finish last in the American League. Then Eddie Joost took over the shortstop position and we finished in first division. Joost made the difference. Nothing got past him; some of his catches were practically miraculous. The whole team was "sparked up" by Eddie's brilliant playing, and the other members of the team played up to Joost's standard, with the result that the standing of the Athletics at the end of the season surprised nearly everybody.

[SECOND BASE AND SHORTSTOP]

Now although a big physique is not an absolute requirement for these two positions, there are certain fundamentals that both shortstop and second baseman MUST have. First, they must be lightning fast on their feet. Second, they must have big hands. I always look closely at the hands of a candidate for either of these two positions to make sure that they can handle all kinds of balls, whether hit or thrown, with absolute certainty.

Extremely important in both second baseman and shortstop is quick judgment. Big leaguers in these two spots have to be able to make split-second decisions on which may hang victory or defeat. There can't be any second-guessing when the chips are down and the ball is speeding toward you like an express train. It's that extra added brainpower that has made stars of fellows like Eddie Collins, Marty Marion, Lou Boudreau and the immortal Honus Wagner.

Before you decide to become a second baseman or shortstop, you should learn to field the ball properly. Whenever possible, the ball should be taken in front of the body without breaking stride. The body should be low, with the knees bent and the feet in a comfortable stance. If you keep your body low you will find it easier to jump up quickly to field the ball on an unexpected hop.

A good fielder uses both hands to handle the ball, the gloved hand to catch it and the "meat hand" to close in over it the instant it is trapped in the glove. Whenever possible, trap the ball on or near the ground because it is less likely to get away from you at that level than on the hop. If it happens that you fumble or bobble the ball, retrieve it as quickly as you can with the throwing hand so that you will lose no time in getting it away.

Remember this: In fielding the ball, *keep your eye on it all the time.* Some players, believing they have "sure" catches, look up to survey the diamond for the throw be-

fore the ball is in the glove with the result that they lose the ball. Be sure you have the ball in your hand before you start to throw it.

Many fly balls are hit to the second base area because it is on a direct line with the pitcher and the batter. The best way to handle fly balls is with the arms and hands held well out in front of you but relaxed. If you are sure you can make the catch, call out to the other players who are trying for it so that there will not be a collision. Otherwise everybody may miss the catch and the batter will be safe. One of the rules is that the player who calls for a catch has the right of way.

[SECOND BASE AND SHORTSTOP]

Unlike both first and third basemen, the second baseman straddles the base when he covers it. In that way he makes it unnecessary for himself to go after the runner; the runner is forced to slide into the bag and be tagged. The idea is to catch the ball and hold the gloved hand in which it rests in front of the base. In that way, the defending second baseman can tag any part of the runner's body that comes in close on the inevitable slide.

A very important function of the second baseman is to assist in double plays. This takes real skill and co-ordination because the ball has to be fielded, the baseman has to pivot and the ball has to be thrown all in one continuous movement.

If the ball lands near second base, the second baseman will field it, touch the base and throw to first. Sometimes, the second baseman may tag the runner if the ball is fielded to the right of the base and then complete the throw to first.

When the ball lands on the other side of second base, the shortstop will run over to cover the base and the second baseman will field the ball. The toss to the shortstop should either be underhand in a scooping sort of motion, or a straight throw, depending on the distance from the base at which the ball is stopped.

However, when the ball is hit to the third baseman or shortstop, the second baseman functions as the pivot man on the double play attempt. On this play he charges over from his fielding position, tags the base in stride as he receives the throw, pivots and fires the ball to first base.

In pivoting he attempts to step clear of the runner

who is being forced at second, thus avoiding a collision that might break up the double play attempt.

Of course there are many variations of this play, depending upon the style of the individual second baseman, but the principle is the same: get the ball, touch the base and fire the ball to first in one fast and unbroken movement.

The second baseman also acts as a relay man on long hits to right or to center field. On such occasions, the second baseman drops back into right field and takes the ball from the right or center fielder, relaying it to the infield as the circumstances may dictate. Such a long throw requires a strong throwing arm, not to mention a sense of accuracy in directing the throw.

As I have said before, the functions of the shortstop and second baseman are so much alike that naturally the qualifications needed for one are also needed for the other with the possible exception of the throwing arm, which in the shortstop should be stronger than in the second baseman, if anything.

I know this will sound funny coming from me, but I believe that the truly great baseball players have a sort of extra sense of perception that enables them to tell almost to a certainty where the ball will be hit so that they will be there ready to receive it when it comes.

Some of the great shortstops have had this sense of perception. When you see a line smash driven right into the glove of a waiting shortstop, like Marty Marion, don't think it's entirely accidental. Chances are he KNEW somehow that the ball was going to be driven to that spot and there he was waiting for it.

[SECOND BASE AND SHORTSTOP]

Ordinarily the shortstop plays about thirty feet to the left of second base. The distance may be changed to meet the requirements of the game or in defense against a particular batter, but wherever he stands the shortstop should take a relaxed position leaning slightly forward, the feet about a foot and a half apart and the weight on the balls of the feet.

The shortstop should field the ball in the same manner as described for the second baseman. He must be able to throw from any position with unerring accuracy, as there is often no time for straightening up to throw. On plays when there is plenty of time most shortstops throw overhand, as it is more accurate and easier for the receiver to handle.

Because the shortstop handles so many pop flies and infield flies, this would seem to be a good place to discuss the infield fly rule.

When there are men on first and second, or runners on first, second and third, and there are either none out or one man out, any fly ball that is hit into the infield is an infield fly for an automatic out whether it is caught or not. If only first base is occupied, the infield fly rule does NOT apply. Obviously, if the runners on base know the rule they will not run on an infield fly; if they leave the bases they do so at their own risk.

You may be interested to know why this rule was adopted. Before it was written into the rule books, if a pop fly was hit to the third baseman, runners on first and second would hold their bases so that they would not be doubled off base. The third baseman, by dropping the ball, could then step on his base for an automatic force-out and then throw to second for another out. The rule was therefore adopted to prevent infielders from getting two outs where only one was deserved on a dropped pop fly.

Another function that is filled by both second baseman and shortstop, although you seldom see this from the stands, is the relaying of signals to the outfield and to the first and third basemen, who may not always be in position to see the signals at the plate. This is particularly important, for if the outfielders know what kind of pitch is coming up they will know where to station themselves to receive the ball should it be hit.

The shortstop also has to cover third base in some emergencies. On run-ups, when a runner is trapped between second and third, or between home and third base, and the third baseman has to leave his base, the shortstop covers for him. Again, when a slow bunt is laid down with a man on first, and the third baseman and first baseman are playing in for it, the shortstop covers second, in case there should be a play at second base, while the second baseman covers first.

On plays between third base and short, the third baseman has the call on the ball except where there is a man on second who might break for third. In that event, the shortstop moves in on the play while the third baseman covers his own base to prevent an advance by the man on second base.

On long fly balls to left field, the shortstop acts as a relay man just as the second baseman does for long hits to the right field and right-center. On such occasions, the shortstop goes back about fifty or seventy-five feet, de-

[SECOND BASE AND SHORTSTOP]

pending on the distance the ball has been hit, so that the retriever will not have to throw the ball more than a hundred and fifty feet. The ball should be caught in such a manner that a pivot to the left will put the shortstop in position to throw directly to the intended receiver.

The shortstop spot is one of the most active on the diamond. You see plenty of action there, and when the shortstop and second baseman team up, they can be spectacular. And it is the one area on the diamond where lack of bigness is not a handicap; it offers hope for the fellow who thinks there is no place for him in the major leagues because he's not a six-footer.

THE OUTFIELD

To those who do not fully understand baseball strategy, the value of the outfielders to a ball team is often underestimated. For reasons which are very easy to discern, most young fellows who want to make baseball a career aim for the battery or infield positions; there are very few who deliberately say to themselves: "I want to play in the outfield." And yet on many teams the name of the player who will first come to your mind will be a star outfielder.

Such outstanding sluggers as Joe DiMaggio, Ted Williams, Babe Ruth, Tris Speaker and many others who in their time led their respective leagues in batting were outfielders. That should give you a clue to one important requirement for a good outfielder: he has to be a strong man at bat. Most outfielders do not start their major

[THE OUTFIELD]

league careers at either right, center or left field. A good many of them try for the pitching or catching positions and later shift over to the outfield positions. In fact, Babe Ruth started as a left-hand pitcher and was a good major league pitcher before he was switched to the outfield.

Now this doesn't mean that just because a fellow is a good hitter he is relegated to the outfield. While it is true that much of the play takes place in the infield, the outfielders have to be able to handle the hits that come their way without fail. A ball that is hit to the second or third baseman can momentarily be fumbled and still be whipped over to first base in time for the out, but an outfielder has to field the ball perfectly because of his distance from the bases and the time it takes to throw the ball back.

That should give you additional clues to the requirements of a good outfielder. He has to be fast and must have a good throwing arm.

When you sit in the stands and see only an occasional ball hit to the outfield you get the mistaken idea that an outfielder doesn't have to work hard. Nothing can be further from the truth. Over the course of a season an outfielder may have an average fielding record of a little more than three chances per game, which doesn't sound like much. Every outfielder, however, has the responsibility of covering certain territory. Look at the baseball field and you will see how it fans out from the plate. You will observe that the infielders each have a specified territory that they must cover, but because they are in close to the plate, their individual territories are not as large as those assigned to the outfielders. When you get to the outfield the three players out there really have ground to cover and for this they need good strong legs and plenty of speed. Undoubtedly, some of the most spectacular running catches are made in the outfield.

It used to be that a manager would be content to take a man on for his outfield if he was a terrific hitter and only a mediocre fielder, but that is no longer the case. To play in the outfield on a major league club today a man must be a power hitter, an outstanding thrower and a speedy runner. The introduction of the lively ball into big league baseball has made these requirements imperative.

The outfielder has to be a crack fielder. Many outfielders get their initial fielding experience in the infield; they also learn what the plays are likely to be, and when they go to the outfield this preparatory course is of great value.

Judgment also counts for a great deal in the outfield because there are many factors which affect play in the outfield to a much greater extent than they affect infield play.

For example: the condition of the turf in the outfield has a great influence on the play. If the ground is soft the ball is not apt to bounce as high or as far as it would if the ground were hard and dry. Then, too, if the ground is soft the ball is apt to roll in the grass instead of bouncing. This will affect the manner of fielding. The outfielder also has to be aware of wind currents and directions, which may shift several times during the course of a game. He also has to have good vision so that the

[THE OUTFIELD]

shadows and the sunlight that generally prevail during the afternoon will not cause him to become confused and lose a ball that has been hit into the air.

Good vision is important in an outfielder for another reason: he must always be aware of what is happening in the infield. The type of pitch to be thrown is signaled to the outfield on every toss so that the outfielders can station themselves accordingly. In order to catch a signal that is being given him by an infielder who holds his hands behind his back, an outfielder who may be as much as 150 feet away has to be able to see it clearly. Otherwise the signal is of no value.

Of the three outfielders the center fielder probably has to be the speediest. Because he is in direct line with the pitcher, catcher and batter, more long hits go to him than to the other two outfielders. A general rule in handling the outfield is that if the center fielder can take the ball he usually does so. The center fielder also backs up the second baseman.

The right fielder is the outfielder who needs the strongest arm of the three because he sometimes has to make one of the longest throws on the field, from right field to third base.

The left fielder ordinarily is busier than the right fielder on defensive play because there are more right-handed batters than southpaws. Consequently, there are more hits into left field than into right.

In planning outfield strategy, the three are considered as a unit. The center fielder is the pivot man. When a man who hits into left field is at bat, I generally signal the center fielder to move over toward left field. Correspondingly, the left fielder will move further right and the right fielder will come in until he is a short distance to the left of the ordinary position that would be taken by the center fielder. For a batter who ordinarily hits into right field I wave my score card in the other direction to give the center fielder the signal and, of course, the other two outfielders move along with him.

There are two types of hits that have to be handled by outfielders, the long fly ball and the ground ball. Add to these an occasional heavy hit ball that bounces off the fence or sidewall of a grandstand. These latter, however, are few and far between. Let's take up the fly ball first.

The most important thing in handling balls hit to the outfield is to get a fast start. For that reason you will always find a big league outfielder constantly on his toes. On a fly ball he MUST get to the spot where the ball will fall before the ball gets there or the batter will have hit safely. Now you can see for yourself how many factors are involved in catching a fly ball. Obviously, the outfielder is going to have to run to the spot where the ball may be expected to land and he will have to run at considerable speed, so he must judge distance and relative speeds; he must also keep his eye continually on the ball if he can, and he must catch it in such a way that he is prepared without any loss of time to throw it back to whatever spot the situation requires.

The minute the pitcher starts his windup the outfielders should take the "ready" stance. The body is bent slightly forward, the feet should be about 18 inches apart and the body weight should rest on the balls of the feet. From this position the outfielder can break quickly

[THE OUTFIELD]

in whatever direction the flight of the ball demands. If he has to run he should run with short strides at the start and as he gets momentum he can lengthen his strides. The outfielder will soon learn, if he doesn't already know, that he can run fastest on his toes. The arms should not be brought up into the catching position until he is vir-

tually at the spot where the ball is going to drop. It will help in gaining momentum if the arms are allowed to swing in pretty much the same fashion as they would be held in a foot race.

Many players have their own individual style for catching a ball. Some make the so-called "basket" catch, holding the gloved hand close to the waist or chest and letting the ball drop into the gloved hand. However, whenever possible, I think it best to catch the ball at about face level with the arms extended. The hands should form a cup into which the ball could fall and when the ball hits the glove there should be a little give. As in all other fielding, if the ball is caught below the waist level the cup should be formed by holding the palms outward, the fingers pointing downward. If the ball is to be caught above the waist the palms are turned inward and the fingers pointed up.

One of the few occasions in a ball game where it is permissible to take your eyes off the ball temporarily is when you find that the ball has been hit over your head. As I have already said, one of the cardinal rules of baseball is to keep your eye on the ball, but in order to do so where a ball has been hit over your head you should not run backward. The way to field a fly ball hit considerably behind you is to figure out where the ball might land, turn your back to the ball and run for the spot. It takes a lot of practice to be able to catch a ball over your shoulder. Tris Speaker was a past master of this technique, and because he was never afraid to go back after a ball he was able to play closer to the infield than an outfielder would ordinarily play. Of course, he played every batter individually; I don't mean to imply that he played in close against every batter.

In playing outfield flies judgment counts for much. A man who cannot run as quickly as another may be able to field the ball more speedily because he has used the right judgment in determining where the ball will drop. The idea is to get to the ball as quickly as you can.

Important in the technique of getting to the ball is also

[THE OUTFIELD]

your position after you've got to it. The most advantageous position is to be behind it, for if you are behind the ball you can catch it on the run and get your throw off in the least possible time. Another factor is that when you are behind the ball you are alert to any change in the course of the ball.

Assuming you have reached the spot where the ball is falling and have caught it on the fly, the next thing is to hold on to it. This takes a pair of big and reliable hands; there are occasions when an outfielder may not be able to catch the ball with both hands and has to go for it with his gloved hand, or even with his "meat hand." But no matter what happens, he has to hold on to it.

An outfielder cannot afford to be sluggish or lazy. He has to go after the ball whether he can get it or not. He must try, and keep on trying. I think that one of the most sensational catches ever made on any field was the one that Al Gionfriddo, the Brooklyn Dodgers' utility man, made in the 6th game of the 1947 World Series, when he snared Joe DiMaggio's terrific 415-foot hit by leaning into the center field bullpen. There were two men on base at the time and if he had not held on to the ball it would have gone for a home run and the Yankees would have won the Series then and there. That catch resulted in the Series going down to the last game. I was in the stand when Gionfriddo came up with the ball in his glove and I don't know of any greater thrill I ever got in all my years in baseball.

Now about fielding ground balls: they may be handled in the same fashion as an infielder handles a ground ball. As a matter of fact, I frequently have my outfielders practice in the infield. But here, too, it is important to get a quick start and to know where the ball is going to drop so that it can be handled on one hop.

In the outfield, the course of the ball may demand that it be fielded safely so that it doesn't get away. In that case, instead of bending and catching the ball with the

glove between the legs, the outfielder should drop to the ground on one knee. The catch should be made in this position; if the ball gets away it can be blocked with the legs or some other part of the body.

Naturally, the main idea after you have fielded the ball is to throw it back to the infield as swiftly as possible, either to a relay man or direct to a base in order to attempt to catch a runner. This calls for fast action but at

[THE OUTFIELD]

no time should you ever throw the ball back without knowing where you are throwing it and without having control of the throw. The most effective method of throwing is overhand, using the same grip on the ball that the pitcher uses for his fast ball. It is a mistake for an outfielder to try to throw the ball to the infield with any other than the overhand toss.

Of course, this doesn't apply to a relay or a very short throw which can be met as the situation warrants. I am talking about long throws in an attempt to make an out.

In every case the outfielders should have worked out a plan of strategy in advance. They should know the batter and the type of pitch that is about to be thrown. They should be prepared for the kind of play that might become necessary if the ball is hit to the outfield. They must constantly keep abreast of the game, knowing the score, the number of outs, how many men are on base, if any, and the count on the batter; that is to say, how many strikes he has against him and how many balls in his favor.

It goes without saying that against a power hitter the outfielders play deep; against a weaker batter or a batter who is intent on placement rather than distance they play close. For left-handed batters the right fielder plays deep, and for right-handed batters the left fielder goes back.

Outfielders are constantly studying opposing batters to determine their strength and weaknesses and their individual peculiarities. Very often they will confer in the clubhouse with the pitcher and catcher before the game to decide on strategy. Another function of the outfielders is to back one another up, because no matter how sure a man is of catching a ball something may happen unexpectedly which necessitates another player's going after it. In any event, where two outfielders are attempting to field the same ball, they should let each other know by shouting which one is to take it. This prevents collisions and confusion which may result in an advantage to the other team.

Outfielders also have to back up throws from any part of the infield to the bases. For example, the center fielder usually backs up throws to second base, the right fielder backs up first and the left fielder third. A fast outfielder also will run to back up a run-down with the left fielder backing up third base, the right fielder backing up first base, and the center fielder backing up second base.

An outfielder should always keep his arm in good throwing shape. Throws from the outfield have to be swift and sure because they travel a greater distance and therefore take longer to reach their target. This may be only a second or two, yet that second may be a crucial one. If the outfielder cannot rifle the ball in, any runners on bases will feel free to take longer leads than they might otherwise take. While it is true that the outfielders are expected to compensate in some measure by strength of batting, they cannot afford to let down on their throwing, and unless you have a strong, accurate throw which is always under control, you will have difficulty in becoming a major-league outfielder.

There is a basic strategy in connection with playing in the outfield and it may be well to set forth these elements right here.

If a single is hit to the outfield and there are none out

[THE OUTFIELD]

and no runners on base, the throw should be to second base, not to first.

If there is a runner on first and there are no outs or only one, on a hit to the outfield the ball should be thrown to second base. Of course, under certain circumstances, if the ball is fielded by the center fielder the throw might be to third to catch the man running from first, but the safe play is to hold the batter at first by throwing to second.

If there is a runner on second, regardless of the number of outs, on a base hit to the outfield the throw should be to the plate. If there is no chance to catch the runner at home the pitcher will intercept the ball and throw it to second to try to put out the runner who may be coming down from first.

One fundamental point in throwing from the outfield is that the ball should be thrown not more than 10 feet off the ground. In this way you will get more speed on the ball and on a long throw it will bounce or hop.

The best strategy in playing the outfield is to let the hitter have one base rather than two or three or even four by being over-anxious and thereby muffing the play completely. The idea is to stop the ball at all costs if you can, even if you have to fall on it.

Don't get the idea that because every ball isn't hit to the outfield, these positions are not important. It is the long hit that will count most against you if you fail to catch it or retrieve it in time to prevent runs from scoring.

BASE RUNNING

It seems to me that a great deal of the excitement that used to pervade a baseball game twenty-five or thirty years ago is somehow missing. There is an explanation for this: With the advent of the livelier ball, the emphasis is on power and longer hitting rather than on speed around the bases.

A big-league player no longer has to be a ten-second man, although running still rates as one of the three essentials of the game. He depends now on the distance of his hit to give him the time necessary to reach the base he aims for rather than his fleetness afoot.

Today the fellow who combines the ability to hit with skill in base running and more particularly base stealing gets the top headlines. In the old days it was Ty Cobb who led the pack in stolen bases; in fact, after Jackie Robinson's first big-league base-stealing episode with the

[BASE RUNNING]

Brooklyn Dodgers, he was compared with the incomparable Ty.

There have been many great base-stealers in my day—Eddie Collins, who played with the Athletics; Max Carey, Pete Reiser and that Wild Horse of the Osage, Pepper Martin, who invariably came in head first (which I do not recommend to you). But of them all, I think Cobb was the greatest.

He was the living example of what a great player's reputation could do to his opponents. Ty's base-stealing ability was not only respected but feared as well; when he was on base, which was very often, his opponents were very apt to be a little more on edge than usual.

One day the Detroit Tigers were playing the St. Louis Browns, then managed by my old friend Branch Rickey. The score was tied and Detroit was coming to bat in the last half of the ninth inning. Cobb was the lead-off man. He walked.

Now Cobb used to take one of the biggest leads in the major leagues—about 20 feet off base. He used to say a lead was no good if you didn't have to slide to get back to base.

Instead of playing the batter, the Browns' pitcher tried four times to pick Cobb off at first because of the long lead he took, and each time Cobb stretched it a little further toward second. On the return of the fourth throw to the pitcher, Cobb headed for second—and made it!

The pitcher's throw was wild, so Ty dashed for third. The ball was in the third baseman's hand before Cobb got there, but Ty slid into him feet first and knocked the ball from his grip.

He was on his feet in a second, flashing toward home. The third-sacker retrieved the ball and pegged it to the catcher, who lunged out to meet the onrushing Tiger. But Cobb slid home with a hook slide, got past the catcher to touch a corner of the plate with one spiked foot and ended the game with the winning run. He had stolen three bases.

I don't recall this having been done by any other player in the major leagues. But of course, there has never been another Tyrus Raymond Cobb.

While speed on foot is a highly desirable asset in a baseball game, you must remember that the best base runners are not always the fastest. They are, however, sometimes the smartest. For equally important with speed are the ability to get a quick start and the ability to think quickly, to make decisions in a flash. And you have to be very observant because in actual contests everything happens in split seconds and you must be guided by your observations, as I will show.

Many games, and important ones at that, have been lost because a base runner neglected to play it safely or because he was negligent in some other aspect of his run around the bases, such as failing to tag the base, or heading for a base already occupied by a teammate.

One of the classic incidents of this type in baseball history occurred one afternoon in 1926 when the Brooklyn Dodgers were playing the Boston Braves at Ebbets Field and somehow or other after a long, long hit by Babe Herman which would ordinarily have been a triple, with the bases filled, there were three Dodgers resting on third base—Dazzy Vance, Chick Fewster and Babe Herman.

[BASE RUNNING]

Vance had been on second, Fewster on first. The man on third had scored. Vance had gone to third and held up. Fewster had gone to second, intending to go to third, but seeing Vance hold up, did likewise. Herman, however, so intent on getting around the bases, failed to see Fewster as he passed him at second, and almost beat Vance into

third. That is another base-running play that stands unmatched in major league history.

The moral of that story is: When you're running the bases, keep your eyes open!

When do you start running? The instant you hear the crack of the bat against the ball.

The big-league player learns to take off with the impact of bat and ball without waiting to see whether the ball is foul or fair, whether it is a fly or a grounder, whether it is an easy out or a home run. He runs out every hit at full speed.

Very often instinct tells you that a batted ball will easily be scooped up by an infielder and tossed to first base for the out. Yet there is a chance that the infielder will bobble the ball, or maybe miss it altogether, and if you run at full speed you can land safely at first.

The quick start is important. The idea is to pivot, immediately after hitting the ball, and push off with the hindmost foot. The first step toward the initial sack should be taken with the front foot, and the run should carry on in an unbroken stride to the base.

When you get to first base, don't leap into the bag. In your regular stride touch the base. Be ready to make a quick break for second in case of an overthrow or an error at first. You are the best judge as to whether you can make it.

On any kind of a hit, the batter should "make the turn" at first base by pivoting toward second. This is done by touching the inside corner of the base with the left foot and turning at the same time so that the right foot will be pointing in the direction of second base.

It is important that the "turn" be made in stride. Some leading hitters start their dashes for first on the other side of the foul line. There is nothing in the rule book against this, provided the player is not attempting to avoid being put out. About two-thirds of the distance from home plate you should describe a small arc and turn sharply toward second.

[BASE RUNNING]

This enables you to touch the bag and still be headed in the direction of second base.

Once you are safe on first, find out who has the ball. If you don't know, plant yourself smack on the bag and look around until you find out. Otherwise your opponents may work the hidden-ball trick on you, and in all my sixty-seven years in baseball I have never known

TO 2ND BASE

TOUCH INSIDE CORNER OF BASE FOR THE TURN

a player to look as foolish as he does after the hidden ball has been brought out of its hiding place to tag him out.

The best plan is to watch the pitcher. He is not allowed to step into the pitcher's box unless he has the ball. If he shifts around on the mound, going everywhere except into the box, you can be sure there's a good reason. To be in the box he has to have his foot on the rubber—remember that, ON the rubber. If he goes into the box without the ball in his possession, he has committed a balk and you will be entitled to take second. So keep your eye on the pitcher until you're sure he has the ball.

In base running, and particularly in stealing bases, the most important tactic is getting a lead. An average lead on a right-handed pitcher is about 12 feet; on a left-handed pitcher about 9 feet. Of course, some big-leaguers take longer leads; Jackie Robinson sometimes takes leads up to 20 feet.

The individual player himself has to be the judge of how long a lead he will take. He has to know—and can learn only from practice—how far off base he can go with reasonable assurance that he can get back safely if the catcher pegs to the base, or that he can get back in time to tag up and beat the relay to second if a fly ball is hit to the outfield.

If you take a lead off the base, the body should be kept low, with the weight on the balls of the feet. By keeping the arms loose and moving them back and forth lightly, you can keep "steam up" in the event you have to break for second base in a hurry.

But you must never take your eyes off the pitcher, for his motions are the trigger that will set you off. You have to watch every part of his body, his arms, shoulders, feet and knees, to ascertain the split second when the pitch is going to leave his hand. That is the instant when you must start running.

Don't look back, in the middle of the steal, to see whether the ball is being thrown toward you. If you will watch the baseman guarding the base you are trying to steal, you will be able to judge where he is going to catch the ball.

[BASE RUNNING]

There is little to be gained in attempting to steal a base if your team is far behind. The time when a stolen base counts is when your team is a run behind, or the game is tied, and you hit safely or are walked to first base with one man out. In that case, by making second base, you can score the winning or tying run on a base hit to the

outfield. That's when a stolen base counts.

A good base runner is as adept off his feet as on them. By that I mean that a good base runner has to know how to slide most efficiently. This is another phase of baseball that used to be most exciting and spectacular but has been eclipsed by the long hit. But every major-league player should know how to slide safely.

It is unfortunate, but also undeniable, that among players of less experience, most baseball injuries result from attempts to slide. Most of these injuries come because the player starts his slide too late. A good many inexperienced players start to slide about five feet from the base. This is like trying to bail out of a plane with a parachute at 50 feet. You'll land pretty hard; that's what happens when you delay your takeoff on a slide. You hit the base pretty hard, and if your legs and feet get tangled up with either the sack or the defending baseman, someone's apt to get hurt.

There are a number of types of slide: The head-first slide, which probably exposes the runner to the greatest risk of injury; the feet-first slide, in which the runner slides into the bag with both feet together, and the "hook" slide, which is the one most often used today.

Sliding is generally employed only on a close play. It is used when a player is trying to avoid being tagged by a defending baseman and also to keep from overrunning the bases beyond first. The slide should never be toward the baseman, but away from him. But you must remember one thing: Once you have made up your mind to slide and have committed yourself to the action, you MUST slide.

A slide that you attempt to cut short before completion can lead to injury, particularly if your spikes catch the bag or the dirt and buckle your leg while your full weight is on it.

Now let me tell you how to steal a base using the "hook" slide. Suppose you are coming in to second base on a close play. You keep your eye on the baseman, for by so doing you can tell on which side of the base he is going to catch the ball. This determines your own course of action, for you must always hook your slide to the side

[BASE RUNNING]

of the bag opposite to the one on which he is standing to receive the throw.

The idea obviously is to expose as little of your body to the tag as possible and to make him reach for it as far as possible.

Suppose you wanted to slide to the right of second base. About 10 or 15 feet from the bag you would take a

position which would bring your body to the ground with the weight on the upper right leg. The torso would be inclined backward with the head and shoulders up. The idea is to go down at an angle, not in a horizontal jump at the base. Both right and left legs are bent.

As the slide is made, the instep of the left foot should hook the base while the body falls away somewhat to the right of the bag.

The slide to the left is the same in principle, only with

the movements reversed. Because only one foot is near enough to the baseman to be tagged, the danger of spiking is minimized when this slide is used.

Thirty years ago, base runners used to try to kick the ball out of the baseman's glove while making a hook slide. There was no rule against this and it sometimes worked. It isn't done much today because a good infielder guards against this trick. It's not considered sporting baseball.

Risky as the slide may seem to be, it is still less dangerous than coming to a sudden stop after running at full speed. Such a sudden stop may result in a rupture. For that reason, and since a runner is not permitted to overrun second and third bases, I always advise my players to hit the dirt on force plays into second and third.

Stealing home is probably one of the most thrilling of all baseball plays but it is all too seldom attempted, first because the circumstances that justify the attempt are seldom present and second, because the probability of getting away with it is not too great.

If you are on third, with two out and a weak hitter at bat, you might just as well try to steal home and score a run by taking a lead, and scuttling for the plate just as the pitcher takes his eye off you to deliver the pitch, or at the instant the catcher snaps his wrist on the return throw to the mound.

Of course, there is plenty of strategy to base running. Base running has its own signals, which are relayed from batter to base-runner, or from coach to player. The runner also has the assistance of the coaches, who tell him what to do. A runner at second or third base is directed

[BASE RUNNING]

by the third-base coach; at first base, the runner takes instructions from the coach back of first base.

The strategy is apt to change with every ball that is pitched. For that reason I stress again one very important requirement for a big-league base-runner: he must know everything that is going on in the game when he is on base, and to do so, he must keep his eyes open and his wits about him. And he must run out every hit; many a supposed infield out has developed into a safe hit. And it's the hits that win ball games!

TEAM PLAY

BASEBALL is played by teams, not by individuals. It is inevitable that in the course of a game or a season or even over a period of years certain players will be outstanding on offense or defense or both. The names that get into the headlines are those of the heavy hitters or champion base stealers or those who stand out in spectacular play. But no one man ever won a baseball game by himself. Behind him were not only the eight men on the playing field but the substitutes, the pinch-hitters, the coaches and, if I may modestly say so, the manager.

Because baseball is a team game there has to be an agreement beforehand as to how the game is to be played against a particular opponent. Every man on the Athletics' team, for example, and this holds true of all major league teams, constantly watches the actions of players on all opposing teams and, when the strategy is being

[TEAM PLAY]

planned for any particular game, everyone contributes what he has observed to the general discussion. Generally the critical decisions are made by the manager of the team, but don't think that the manager makes every decision all by himself. Very often a good manager will consult with a player who is in a position to have special knowledge of the opposing team or the opposing batter before he makes his decision.

Team play comes into action on offense as well as defense. Some would-be ball players get the erroneous idea that the way to win ball games is entirely through hitting. That may be true if the other side isn't hitting, too. So in addition to trying to score runs on offense the game also calls for defense to prevent the other side from scoring.

I believe that both phases of baseball are equally important. But in each you must have a team that is harmonious and well adjusted. You cannot have a winning ball club where there is dissension and divided loyalty. Nor can you have a winning team when there is envy or jealousy of one or two men because they happen to be outstanding.

The great ball teams of history have always been those where the friendliest relationships prevailed between the individual players and where there was present that most essential element called "team spirit."

The hub of defense in baseball, the focal point around which all action revolves and the fellow upon whom the play depends is the pitcher. He cannot, however, win the game all by himself, although there is a story that a very famous hurler who once played for the Athletics did not need the outfield to support him. I am sure you have heard of the great and erratic Rube Waddell, who pitched for the Athletics in the early days of the century. He was one of the greatest strike-out artists in the game.

I sometimes still hear stories of how Rube would call in the outfielders in the ninth inning and indicate that he was going to strike out the next three batters. That sometimes happened, but not in scheduled season games. Then, as now, the Athletics, like all major league teams, played exhibition games before the beginning of the regular season and in some of those exhibition games Waddell would motion the fielders to come in and go either to the bench or to the showers. With only one man in the field to play first base he would proceed to strike out three batters in a row. As a matter of fact, in 1904 Rube struck out 343 batters in league play, a record that stood until Bobby Feller broke it in 1946 with 348 strikeouts.

The pitcher's first assistant is the catcher. Following the catcher come the second baseman and shortstop. After them, the center fielder. You will notice that all these five play virtually in a line if you consider the second baseman and the shortstop as interchangeable parts of a playing unit. This is the axis around which the whole defense revolves. The other players are flankers to the main axis, and when you play game strategy you start with the axis as the main basic defense; you bring the flankers into play when the game calls for a variation in the defense.

Now I don't want to give the impression that every bit of play is preordained and scheduled in advance, because if that were so, the individual play would not count at all.

[TEAM PLAY]

That isn't so. Every particular move is up to the individual. If you are playing in the outfield and a fly ball is hit into your territory, it is you who have to catch it. Your team mates will back you up if you should happen to miss the ball or drop it. If you are at bat, it is you who have to hit the ball; the manager or the coaches may tell you, via signals, the kind of pitch to expect, but they cannot hit the ball for you. *That* is up to you.

If you watch a top-notch ball team in action you will observe that all the players with the exception of the pitcher and catcher do not take the same positions in defending against every batter. If they did and the opposing team got wise to the fact I doubt if the defending team could ever win a game. But because the whole team has to be prepared to meet any situation that comes up, the players have to shift as a unit. Merely moving a third baseman over to play against a fellow who has a tendency to hit down the third-base line is not enough. The other players in that particular area, the shortstop, the left fielder and the center fielder all have to shift accordingly in case the batter should hit toward left but away from the third-base foul line.

If you have a batter who tends to hit toward right field, the first baseman, second baseman and right fielder would play closer to the first-base foul line so that the unit would be prepared for anything that might happen. Incidentally, Babe Ruth used to hit in that general direction; as a result, when the Babe was at bat, I would motion the players to cover the right side of the field. The trouble with my strategy there, however, was that the Babe would sometimes get the kind of pitch he liked

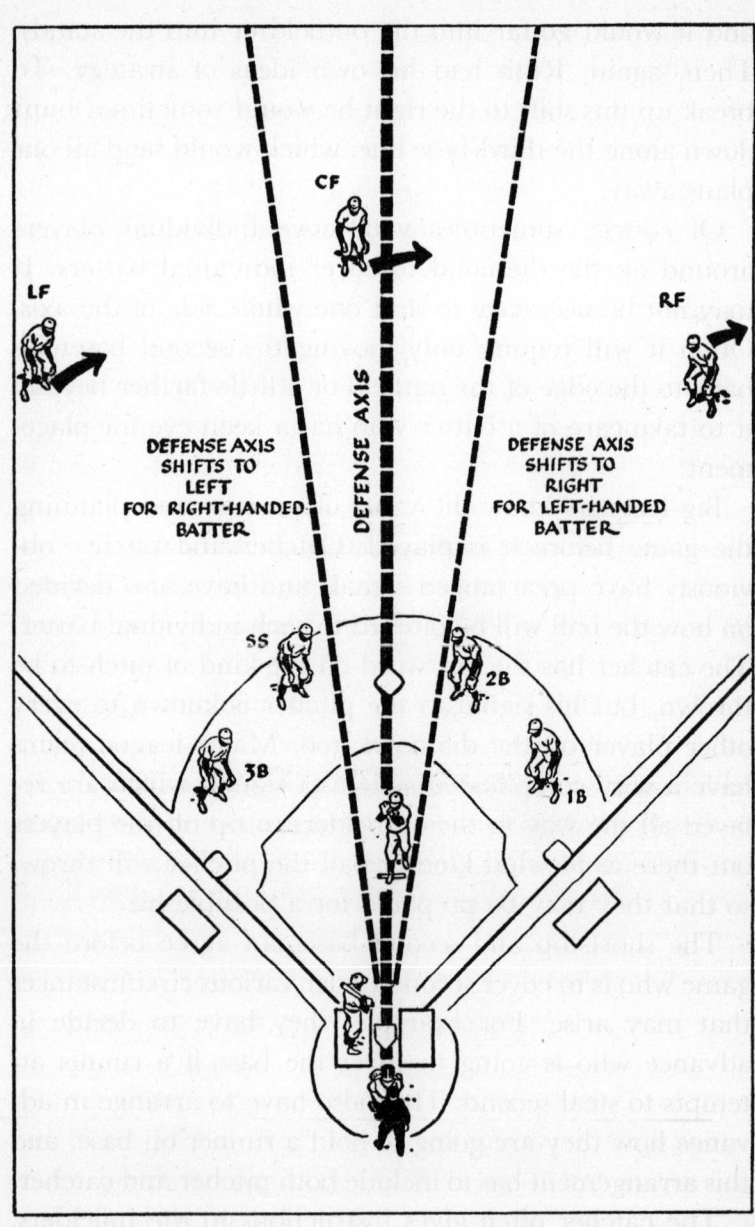

[TEAM PLAY]

and it would go far into the outfield or into the stands. Then, again, Ruth had his own ideas of strategy. To break up this shift to the right he would sometimes bunt down along the third-base line, which would send all our plans away.

Of course, sometimes you move individual players around on the diamond to cover individual batters. It may not be necessary to shift one whole side of the axis. Often it will require only moving the second baseman back to the edge of the outfield or a little farther beyond it to take care of a batter who has a keen eye for placement.

Big leaguers know the value of strategy and planning the game before it is played. Catcher and pitcher obviously have prearranged signals and have also decided on how the ball will be pitched to each individual batter. The catcher has the last word on the kind of pitch to be thrown, but his signal to the pitcher is known to every other player on the diamond, too. Major league teams have a very complicated system of signals which are relayed all the way to the outfielders to tip off the players out there as to what kind of ball the pitcher will throw, so that they may be prepared for a possible hit.

The shortstop and second baseman agree before the game who is to cover second under various circumstances that may arise. For example, they have to decide in advance who is going to cover the base if a runner attempts to steal second. They also have to arrange in advance how they are going to hold a runner on base, and this arrangement has to include both pitcher and catcher.

The catcher often gives instructions to the infielders,

particularly the first baseman and third baseman, by shouting to them, or through a special set of signals, since the first and third basemen are not in a position to see the signals that the catcher gives to the pitcher in his crouching position at the plate.

There are hundreds of situations that could come up in the course of a baseball game where team play is indicated. Take fly balls, for example, that go out into that No-Man's-Land between the infield and the outfield. Such a situation involves three or four men at a time. These players all have to know by prearrangement who will be expected to take the catch within a prescribed area. If there is no prearrangement they have to keep each other informed by shouting during the course of that particular play which one is to handle it. Without such co-operation and team play the ball might drop to the ground, as it sometimes does when the required team play is not present, with bad results to the defending team.

Incidentally, on a play of that kind the rule is that the outfielder nearest the ball takes the catch if he can. Generally the infielder would have to move back to make such a catch while the outfielder has the ball in front of him, and it is always best to come up for a catch rather than to go back for it. However, when he is sure that he can handle it, the outfielder should call out to the other players that he will take it, and when he does so it is up to them to get out of range and leave him a clear field.

The trouble is that occasionally some outfielders forget to let the other players know that they will handle the ball, and with three or four fast men all running at full speed to one spot, collisions sometimes result and the ball falls safe.

The fundamental rule is that every player has to know what is required of him when he goes out on the field. He has to be in the right place at all times and that place shifts with the circumstances of the game. His function on the field is to recover the ball if it should be hit to him or near him. He also has to know what to do with it if he gets it.

A player recovering a ball need not always throw it. Sometimes it is to the advantage of the defending team that the ball be held rather than thrown. Players should remember that every time a ball is thrown, particularly if they are in a hurry and if the thrower doesn't have full control of the ball, there may be an overthrow or an error. Then again, there is no use in trying to make a play that good judgment should tell you in advance cannot be made.

I generally spread my infield players as far apart as possible, especially when the loss of a run will not mean the loss of the game. With a man on third, when one run means the game, I move my infield in so as to cut off the run at home plate.

Team play is also important in catching runners off base. This activity is generally restricted to infielders, although right and left fielders may come in to back up basemen who have left their bases to make run-ups.

The general rule is that three men co-operate in playing men off base. Every time the ball is thrown by one player to another, the fellow who throws moves into the spot previously occupied by the one to whom he is throwing. For example, suppose a runner leaves first base in an attempt to steal second. Either the pitcher or the second baseman will run to first to cover that base, and the shortstop covers second and receives the throw from first. The first baseman will try to get between second base and the runner in an effort to trap him. The runner stops, pivots and turns toward first again for the out. Actually, the out may be made by the second baseman; the runner is generally caught at the base from which he started to run. Meanwhile, under the general defense plan, the first baseman may find himself covering second base, and the center fielder will have come in to back up the shortstop. If a runner on second makes a break for third, the ball is thrown to the third baseman, who then participates in the run-up toward second, while the player who threw to the third baseman goes to third to protect that base.

Where a runner breaks for home from third base, the third baseman will chase him toward the catcher, while the shortstop will move over to third base. On plays like this the catcher will run as far as he can after the runner toward third base and then toss the ball to the shortstop, who will make the out. The third baseman meanwhile will go all the way to the plate to protect it against the run scoring.

On offensive strategy, while there are many situations that come up where defense planning is required, one of the most important factors is the batting order. Of course, if all nine men on the team are excellent hitters and there is little to choose between them in that department, the manager doesn't have any great problem with his batting order. But as anybody who has followed baseball for any

[TEAM PLAY]

period of time knows, there is no such team. Some players are better batsmen than others and the manager has to shift and juggle his batting order in line with certain principles of offensive strategy. You generally pick for your lead-off batter a player who has a quick eye for a pitched ball. He should also be a good bunter and a fast base runner because strategy calls for him to get to first

RELATIVE BATTING ORDER STRENGTH

base if he can. This spot calls for a fellow with excellent control so that if the pitcher has not yet found the range, he can outwait him and get a walk. The lead-off man should preferably not be a heavy hitter, because those who come to bat before him in the usual batting order are those who are the weakest at the plate and are therefore not apt to be on base when the lead-off man comes up during the course of the game.

The second man in the batting order should be a player who can control the direction of his hit. Very often the second man in the batting lineup is called on to sacrifice so that the lead-off man, if he has reached first base, has an opportunity to get to second and thereby be in a scoring position. He should either bunt or use the hit-and-run play and is generally a "choke" batter, laying the ball down precisely where he wants it. I don't mean that he need not be a good hitter; on the contrary, the second man up should be a first-class batsman.

The next two men to come up should be power hitters. These are the fellows who will account for the runs. If the lead-off man has been able to get to first and has been sacrificed to second by Batter Number Two, a hit into the outfield or a long fly ball can score the man from second.

The next batter in the lineup should also be a hard hitter. Assuming that Batters Number Three and Four have been able to land on base, a power hitter in Number Five position will be effective in running up the score. It is very seldom, however, that a manager has been able to obtain a team that is so well balanced in every department of baseball that he can line up three power hitters one after the other.

The man who bats in Number Six position in the lineup should have somewhat the same batting ability as the lead-off man except that he should probably be a somewhat stronger hitter in order to drive in any men who may be on base when he comes to bat. The players who have come to bat before him have presumably been the top hitters of the team, and there is a possibility that one of them will have got on base. In that event Batter Number Six should have some power behind him, either to advance the base runner or perhaps to bring him home.

[TEAM PLAY]

The seventh batter fulfills the same function as the second man in the lineup. He should preferably be a "choke" hitter able to control the placement of the hit, with special ability to handle the hit-and-run play.

Have you ever wondered why the last two men in the batting order are usually the pitcher and catcher? I have been asked that question many times during the years. Well, the real reason is not that the pitcher and the catcher are the weakest hitters on the team, because very often they may be excellent hitters. For example, Lou Brissie is a dependable man at the plate as well as on the mound, and although in the selection of a pitcher you don't stress his batting ability as much as his throwing capacity, very often a young fellow will come up who can both pitch and bat very well.

No, the real reason why the pitcher and catcher are at the foot of the batting order is that they don't play regularly every day, and if the pitcher or catcher were to be put in any other position except Eight and Nine in batting order, it would mean that the regular batting order would have to be changed every day.

Every one of the seven men in the batting order ahead of the pitcher and catcher knows all there is to know about the fellow who comes to bat before him or who follows him at the plate and he bases his play accordingly. If this order were to be changed every time the battery changed, it would be virtually impossible to achieve any co-ordinated offensive strategy, as you can see.

The general principle is to try to get a man on base before bringing up the heavy guns, because if the Number One man should land on base and the Number Two man should fail to advance him through a sacrifice, there are still two or perhaps three heavy hitters concentrated in a group who may be able to bring the Number One man home.

Offensive strategy, which calls for scoring of runs, is based on these principles: that the lead-off man in every inning get to first base, either on a hit or by a walk. Because the batter will be trying to outwait the pitcher on the first pitched ball, the pitcher will inevitably make every effort to put it over the plate. Although the tendency is for the batter to let the first one go by, I have found it very effective to instruct Athletics' players to swing at the first one. It may sound unorthodox, but it sometimes pays off.

Incidentally, that is one of the interesting things about baseball. There are a lot of unwritten rules that have developed as a result of years of experience. And I have found that if, every once in a while, you close the book and play as your judgment dictates, the results are occasionally very surprising.

COACHING, TEAM SIGNALS AND SCORING

THERE are two men in every major league baseball game who are not actually on the official diamond but are as important as anyone who is.

Generally they are older men, players past their playing prime, but very well versed in the strategy of baseball.

If you credit the manager with being the general of the team, the coaches are his lieutenants, for one of their principal functions is to relay strategic instructions from the manager on the bench and keep the attack rolling.

Some of the finest players in baseball graduate to the first and third base coaching boxes. Now don't get the idea that these two spots are pastures to which old baseball players retire. On the contrary, the first and third base coaches have very important responsibilities and are very often the architects of victory.

By this time you have read a lot about players receiving signals and have probably wondered how the batter can get signals which are being given by the manager on the bench, to whom he naturally has his back.

Well, that's where the coaches come in. The coach on the first-base line gives the batting signals to right-handed batters; the coach on the third-base line gives the batting signals to left-handed batters.

You must often have wondered, too, as you watched a big-league game, why the two coaches at first and third seemed so nervous and jittery, moving around a great deal, stooping to pull up wisps of grass or some earth to rub between their hands, or adjusting some part of their uniforms.

True enough, they may be somewhat nervous by temperament—the responsibility that the coaches carry into the game is quite enough to make them nervous—but these outward manifestations are not always to be confused with nervousness. Some of these motions are signals. Through them they are telling the batter, or perhaps a runner on base, or an infielder, what the manager wants him to do under the particular circumstances.

There are very few baseball players who are left to their own devices in action. The strategy of the game is in the hands of the manager; he tells each player what to do by means of signals, and the coach relays these instructions.

[COACHING, TEAM SIGNALS AND SCORING]

But the coach does more than that. Because of his long experience in the game, he is a teacher as well. He studies the players on his team, decides what each one can and cannot do. In practice, in which the coach almost invariably participates, he may offer suggestions for improvement of form to the players.

In action, there are occasions when there is no time to look to the bench for signals; in such cases, as when there is a runner on base and the ball is hit and a decision has to be made instantly whether the runner should try for one base or extras, it is up to the coach to use his own judgment and either send the runner on or tell him to hold up.

The first-base coach, for example, gives the hitter the sign if he is to try to stretch a hit into a two-bagger or more; the third-base coach motions the runner coming from second to hold up at third or to dash for the plate. These are very often important decisions to make; they involve a keen insight into the player's running ability as well as his reaction under pressure. The coaches are very often the most informed men on the field; that is to say, they know most not only about baseball and strategy but also about the players.

The number of signals it is necessary to give are not many; the means employed to give them are countless. Every team has its own set of signals. They are as simple as they can be kept, also highly secret. They are changed frequently, too, because one of the objectives of every player who watches a game from the bench is to try to fathom the signals of his opponents.

Also, a team's signals have to be changed every time one of its players is sold or traded to another team in the league.

Most of the time, signals are given by hand, but they can involve combinations with other parts of the body or

parts of the coach's uniform. For base runners, the signals are simple and out in the open; there is no reason to make a secret of instructions to base runners. These signals are virtually standard and speak for themselves.

When the coach wants the runner to keep on running, he uses a beckoning motion of his left hand, swinging it in to his chest just as you would if you wanted someone to

[COACHING, TEAM SIGNALS AND SCORING]

come closer to you who couldn't hear your shouted instructions.

If the coach wants the runner to hold up on base, he holds up both hands with the palms turned outward as you would if you wanted to tell someone in gestures not

to come closer. If the runner is to attempt to slide safely into the base in order to avoid a throw, the coach gives him the signal by motioning with the hands, the palms being held downward; if the runner is to come into the base standing up, the coach raises his arms above his head.

If a player is to steal a base, he gets the signal for this from the coach; the hit-and-run signal is generally given by the batter.

To the batter the coach conveys two pieces of information: which pitches to strike at and which to let go by or "take"; to describe the exact methods used to convey this information by various coaches of different teams would take another book. The "take" sign might be given with the right hand and the "strike" signal with the left, or vice versa. In giving these signals the cap, or the belt, or some part of the body might be used in combination with the hand, as I have said before.

The object is to keep your signals secret so that your opponents will not get wise to them. For that reason, I

am not going to cite examples of the Athletics' signals, nor am I going to disclose how much we know of our opponents' signals.

This much, however, I can say. Stolen or fathomed signals can sometimes be disastrous, so try to keep your signals secret—but simple.

You must also have wondered as you have watched a major league baseball game why a batter, seemingly poised and awaiting the pitch, suddenly steps out of the batter's box and either adjusts his cap, or taps his heels with the bat to knock the mud out of his cleats.

The chances are his cap hasn't been annoying him nor has the mud in his cleats; the real reason is that he has

[COACHING, TEAM SIGNALS AND SCORING]

either missed the signal the coach is trying to relay to him, or the coach has suddenly cancelled the signal previously given the batter and is telling him to wait until the new signal can be relayed to him from the bench. When the batter steps back into the box, it may be assumed that he has received the new signal.

Obviously the coaches need good eyesight to catch the signals from the bench. Because the bench is below the ground level, it is sometimes difficult for a coach with even 20–20 vision to catch a signal; that's the reason why I use a scorecard to give some of my signals. It can be seen better by the coach and by the players.

By now, however, virtually everyone in the American League knows that I do not give ALL my signals in this way; if I used only this one method the signals would soon become known to our opponents and would thus be rendered valueless.

In addition to the signals given by hand, the coaches also give instructions to base runners by voice. Once a batter has hit the ball, he is supposed to take off for first base and get there as quickly as he can. Some base runners succumb to an irresistible desire to follow the ball with their eyes. This can only have the effect of slowing the runner down, perhaps throwing him off stride. Such a runner will be speeded on his way if the first-base coach shouts: "Come on! Hurry!" or some such expression.

If the runner will leave the watching of the ball to the first-base coach, he can follow the coach's instructions about rounding the base and "making the turn" for second should the opportunity present itself. If the coach sees that the runner has no chance to stretch the hit into a double, he will shout "No! No!" as the man makes the turn.

The first-base coach also watches both pitcher and first baseman for the runner on first base and can warn him if any motion of the pitcher looks suspiciously like an attempt to pick the runner off at first. If the runner has taken a lead, the coach naturally has to give him such a warning by voice.

After the runner passes first base—that is, goes to second or third—he comes under the jurisdiction of the third-base coach. When a runner is rounding second base on a ball hit to right field, the third-base coach has to advise him whether to hold up or to continue on to third and perhaps to the plate. If the coach wants the player to stay on the base and hold up, he will point to the bag with his finger.

The responsibility of the third-base coach is somewhat greater than that of the first-base coach because the third-base coach covers three bases; the first-base coach has only to worry about first. The coach at third has to bear in mind the running speed of his own players and the arm strength of the opposing outfielders and infielders so that he can judge whether his own runner can beat the opponent's throws to base or to the plate; he must also be able to appraise the ability of the batter to hit safely.

In coaching the runner on second base, the third-base coach does so by means of shouted information; he also has to watch the second baseman and shortstop to prevent the runner from being caught off base. As long as these infielders play in their regular spots, the runner is in no danger. If the third-base coach sees either one of

[COACHING, TEAM SIGNALS AND SCORING]

them break for the bag, however, he must shout a warning to the runner to beware of a throw from the plate or the pitcher.

I should like to explain that sometimes a batter is instructed by the manager what to do when he leaves the bench for the "on deck" circle. In that event, the coaches are informed by signals of the instructions given to the batter so that they will know what to expect when he comes to bat.

Another aspect of coaching is conducting the daily warm-up and practice. The coaches not only watch the players in action during the practice session but participate by hitting to the pitchers and to the outfield and infield. They also are responsible for the maintenance of the physical condition of the players, and that brings me to a very important subject.

It is assumed that every young fellow who gets a chance to play in the major leagues is in good condition when he starts. One of the important qualifications for major-league stardom is a good, healthy constitution. As long as you want to continue to play in the majors, you have to keep in good physical condition. And that calls for constant exercise, constant training.

For the better part of forty years, I guess, it has been argued back and forth whether spring training is necessary. In my opinion it is. Particularly for those players who engage in some vocation other than baseball through the winter months—and the vast majority of them do—spring training is essential in getting them back into the good physical condition that is necessary to play a season of highly competitive baseball.

There are many forms of exercise that can be used; I am in favor of the simple ones. The one way to develop running speed, in my opinion, is to run; after you have increased the distance you can run without exhaustion, then increase your speed. Running develops good wind and the muscles of the legs. I also recommend the game of handball as a training exercise because it brings into play the same muscles as are used in playing baseball.

Most difficult to bring into playing condition after a layoff are the pitchers. When the team is practicing, the pitchers who are not actually pitching go to some other part of the field and practice fielding. Pitchers, as a rule, have to be held back in training—that is, they want to bear down in training practice before they are ready. Accordingly, I always caution pitchers at the beginning of the training season not to "pitch their arms out."

If you really want to be a top-notch baseball player, you must always think about your physical condition. You will, if you stop to consider, refuse to do anything that would break your condition down. Don't drink alcoholic beverages or use tobacco. I know that a good many big league players both drink and smoke. Personally, I don't do either. I have made it a rule not to permit smoking on the Athletics' bench while a game is in progress. I realize only too well how difficult it is to keep a young fellow from smoking who has the habit, and I have given up trying to stop my players from smoking off the field. But the best way to control the habit is never to acquire it.

Eat good wholesome food but not too much of it, especially before participating in a game. I eat a heavy breakfast, a very light lunch and another full meal in the evening for dinner. For breakfast I have fruit juice or fresh fruit, eggs, lamb chops, toast and coffee. I drink coffee only once a day—at breakfast.

For lunch I have graham crackers and milk. That's all. But for dinner I have meat, preferably steak, and a full complement to go with it.

No matter what you eat, however, it should be well digested before you go into a game. Because it is unwise to overload the stomach before game-time, a good many players eat very lightly at noon; a bowl of soup or a cup of tea and a sandwich suffice.

There is a danger, however, that in an attempt to eat very little you will not eat enough to give you the strength and endurance that a game demands. Don't undernourish yourself; remember, moderation is the best policy to follow in eating as well as in many other activities in life.

I have touched upon eating and drinking; now a word about sleeping. I believe a person who lives as strenuous a life as a big-league baseball player does during the league season cannot get along with less than eight hours' sleep a night. It takes that much rest to renew the physical strength expended in the course of a game. Some players, during the course of a game played in the hot summer sun, lose as much as ten pounds in an afternoon. A man cannot take that much weight off in the course of a single day without feeling weaker physically. One good way to restore some of this lost strength is through rest.

In practice, don't overdo it. If your muscles begin to feel sore, lay off until they feel better. Don't start your practice like a lion; take it easy and start gently. Be sure your muscles are fully warmed up and loosened before you go into violent exercise. Be sure, also, that you protect the arm and shoulder muscles from wind and cold and rain. You should always have a sweater or windbreaker on hand to wear during any lull either in practice or during a game when you are not in action.

While it is true that a great deal is left to the judgment of the individual scorer, there are some fundamental statistics in scorekeeping that have to be recorded under uniform rules for all teams if they are to be of any value in making comparisons between individual players and the teams themselves.

To compute the players' batting averages, the first thing to know is the number of times they have been at bat. However, under the rules of scoring, a player is not considered to have been at bat if he is walked or hit by a pitched ball, makes a sacrifice hit or is interfered with by the catcher.

It is important that the batting order established before the game be adhered to; if a player is permitted to bat out of turn the error may be very costly. If it is discovered before the pitcher has thrown his first pitch, the batter who should have come up is declared out; if not discovered until after the first pitch, the batter who should have been at bat loses his turn.

Suppose a batter is taken out of the game after he has two strikes against him and the player who comes in in his place takes the third strike. Which one has struck out? The answer is: The first batter. If the player removed had

[COACHING, TEAM SIGNALS AND SCORING]

only one strike against him and the succeeding batter took two more strikes, the strikeout should be charged against the player who was substituting.

A batted ball which a fielder hits with a thrown cap, mask or glove counts as a triple, even if it is a bunt. A thrown ball similarly hit by a thrown cap, mask or glove entitles any runners on base to advance two bases.

For a fair hit to be scored, the batter must reach first base *safely*. Under this rule, if a batter has gone to second on a long hit, but has failed to touch first base while rounding it, he can be called out if the ball is thrown to first, since he did not reach first base *safely*.

I have already referred to the infield fly rule. There is an addition to it: If a runner is struck by an infield fly, the batter is called out. If the runner happens to be standing on base when struck by an infield fly, he is not out; if he is struck while off base, both the batter and the runner are out.

If a hit ball fairly strikes a runner or an umpire or any part of their clothing, the batter is credited with a base hit. The exception to this is the infield fly rule.

In scoring, a batter is never credited with a hit where the play results in a force-out at another base.

Where a thrown ball hits a base runner and he advances an extra base as a result of being hit, the throw is charged as an error against the player who threw it. Similarly where the catcher, trying to catch a runner off base, throws the ball and hits either the batter or his bat, permitting the runner to advance, he is charged with an error.

A pitcher can be charged with an error even though he does not throw the ball to the plate or to any of the bases. Suppose a runner is on base. While waiting to confirm the catcher's signal, the pitcher tosses the ball in the air a few feet, as a good many pitchers do. The ball, instead of falling into his glove, strikes his wrist and falls to the ground. The runner dashes for the next base and makes it safely before the pitcher can throw the ball. Charge an error to the pitcher.

I have often been asked about scoring a hit when the ball *bounces* out of the park. The rule is that if the ball bounces out of the park or is hit into a stand less than 250 feet from home plate, the batter is credited only with a double. This is true even if the ball has been touched by a fielder after the bounce. However, if the ball has not touched the ground, and a fielder, trying to catch it, misses and the ball is deflected off his glove over the fence, the batter is credited with a home run. If it is deflected into a stand less than 250 feet from home plate, it is still scored as a two-base hit.

What about scoring the home run that ends the game in the ninth where the hit comes with a man on base? It is only a home run where the batter drives the ball fairly out of the playing field and *legally touches each base in its proper order*. So on this play, not only does the base runner have to run around the bases, touching each base as he passes it, but so does the hitter, even though the game might be considered actually over when the base runner has tagged home plate after completing the circuit of the bases.

[COACHING, TEAM SIGNALS AND SCORING]

As I have said, scoring a baseball game calls for a judgment on every pitched ball, but over the years I have found that keeping my own score has given much added interest to every baseball game I have watched—and I have lost count of the number.

THE CONTRACT

BEFORE we assume that you have been found by a major league manager to have the ability that will add strength to his team and that he is ready to sign you up, let's think a little about baseball as a profession.

The average ball player does a lot of moving around, not only between cities which have teams in the league in which he plays, but also between leagues. Baseball players are subject to being sold or traded and relatively few get to plant their roots in any particular spot.

The players come from many different backgrounds, from rich families and from poor ones, from farms and coal mines. A chap from the hills of Arkansas may be assigned to the locker next to an urbane city "slicker" from New York when both play on the same team. When the season ends, they scatter to their homes in all parts of

[THE CONTRACT]

the country until it is time to gather for spring training the following year.

So you see, very few baseball players in the major leagues work near their homes.

For many of them baseball is one of two jobs. During the winter they may be employed in some business, may even operate their own establishments from which they derive income in addition to their salaries as ball players.

For the big-league player, baseball is not a business; it is a profession. Like any other occupation involving professional talent, a baseball player gets part of his compensation from his satisfaction in his own athletic ability and accomplishment. His work is not something he merely does perfunctorily but something he loves to do.

The baseball player always has a tremendous incentive to play well, for his future depends on his ability, regardless of the standing of the team on which he plays. He is always in the public eye; people are paying to watch him perform and he feels he is under compulsion to produce.

In baseball there are enormous differences in ability. These differences in individual ability can be seen more easily in baseball players than the differences in skill between actors, let us say, or musicians. The reason for this is that the very competitive nature of baseball automatically provides a means for judging the differences in ability.

You may not be able to agree with a friend about which movie star gave the best performance in a particular film but there can be no question about who was the

[CONNIE MACK'S BASEBALL BOOK]

leading batter in the American League in any year or what third baseman held the best fielding record.

The records are there, uniformly kept, and all you have to do to answer these baseball questions is to look at the records. We may disagree about whether Irving Berlin or George Gershwin is the greater song writer, but as between a ball player with a lifetime batting average of .325 and another in the same league with a .280 standing, there is no doubt as to which one was the better hitter.

Because of these differences in ability, there is always keen competition between players for places on the team —remember, there are only 25 men on each major league team—and there is also keen competition for salaries. A baseball player is paid to produce. It might also be said that he is paid for results, because a player's salary for a particular season is determined largely by his showing and record for the preceding year.

It is largely, though not entirely, true that a baseball player is nearly always a year behind times so far as his pay is concerned since his salary is based considerably on his performance the previous year.

Your pay in major league baseball is fixed by your contract. Of course, you want the most you can get. Sometimes a promising prospect asks for a cash bonus for signing a contract in addition to his salary. Sometimes, too, he gets it. In the major leagues there is no stated top limit on salaries, although Ted Williams' reported $125,-000 a year from the Boston Red Sox is the highest salary for a player I have heard of. There is, however, a bottom salary of $5,000 a year. This is the minimum that a

[THE CONTRACT]

major league club can pay its players. Most first-year men in the majors receive that sum.

Despite what you may hear about the baseball clubs making fortunes, don't believe it. Baseball as a business is very risky; about eighty percent, or four out of five, minor league clubs operate at a loss. Most major league clubs are now operated by wealthy men who are not in it for the money but as a hobby on the part of some, and because of civic pride on the part of others.

To the young fellow who has a chance to get a contract from a major league team and who thinks he ought to hold out for more money than is being offered him, or for a bonus, I say: "Forget it." The big idea is not to make a million dollars your first year in the big leagues but rather to prove that you belong there.

Remember that to get the big money, you have to show that you're worth it.

And another thing: You may get a contract from a big-league team and after a trial period be sent down to the minors for more experience or seasoning.

Baseball is just like any other profession or trade. There are very few individuals who can start at the top. Usually you have to go through a period of apprenticeship and learning; just as in education you go through the primary and grade schools before you get to the institutions of higher learning. The minor leagues are in effect the prep schools for major league competition.

Don't be discouraged by any temporary setbacks. The thing to do is to *prove* that you belong in the upper brackets. Don't turn down a contract because you think it doesn't provide for a high enough salary. If you have the ability that should command a high salary, some day you'll come into your own.

Every player in the major leagues signs the same form of contract, varying only in the amount of salary. It is a four-page printed document, three pages constituting the contract and the fourth page comprising the regulations. Thus, the rights and responsibilities of every player in the major leagues (with the exception of salary) are the same.

Organized baseball now uses the Uniform Players' Contract, which was adopted at the close of the 1947 season. Because I have never seen a copy of the uniform contract printed anywhere in a book or periodical, I am going to give you some of the details of that agreement.

It provides that the player shall receive no less than $5000 a year for his "skilled services" as a team member during the season, including the training season, exhibition games and World Series "or any other official series in which the Club may participate." There is nothing to prevent the player from getting extra compensation from these latter games, however.

The salary is paid in semi-monthly installments after the commencement of the playing season.

If the player is assigned to another duty, or to a club of lower league classification, his salary cannot be cut as long as his contract is in force, and the major league club has to pay any difference between the contract salary and his salary from the minor league club. If he is assigned elsewhere during the season, the club with which he has his contract has to pay his moving expenses up to $500.

[THE CONTRACT]

A player who is injured in the course of his employment under the contract and is released for that reason is entitled to receive his full salary for the year.

If his contract is ended by the club during the training season, the player gets his board, lodging and expense allowance up to the date his contract is ended, plus travelling expenses home.

If the contract is ended during the playing season, the player gets his salary for the number of days he was with the team in proportion to the number of days in the entire season.

All contracts have to be tendered to players on or before February 1st. If the player and the club have not agreed on the contract terms by March 1st, the club has the right to renew the contract for the next year before ten days after March 1st. If it does so, it can fix the player's salary, but the salary cannot be less than seventy-five percent of the previous year's salary.

If a player is hurt in the line of duty, the club pays his medical and hospital bills, up to a reasonable limit.

During the spring training period, the club gives the player an allowance of $25 a week payable in advance, in addition to paying his travelling expenses, board and lodging for the training period. Spring training, by the way, doesn't begin until March 1st under the uniform contract.

Players are now permitted to appear in exhibition games for 30 days after the close of the major league championship season, if the Baseball Commissioner approves.

Those are some of the things the player gets under the

contract. Now what does the baseball club get in return?

One of the first things the player agrees to do is "to perform his services hereunder diligently and faithfully, to keep himself in first class physical condition and to obey the Club's training rules, and pledges himself to the American public and to the Club to conform to high standards of personal conduct, fair play and good sportsmanship."

He also agrees "that while under contract, and prior to expiration of the Club's right to renew this contract, he will not play baseball otherwise than for the Club, except that the Player may participate in post season games under the conditions prescribed in the Major League Rules."

Elsewhere in the contract, the player states that he has "exceptional and unique skill and ability as a baseball player; that his services. . . . are of a special, unusual and extraordinary character which gives them peculiar value which cannot be reasonably or adequately compensated for in damages," and that if the player were to breach the contract, it would cause the club great damage.

He therefore agrees in advance that if he plays for another team while this contract is in force, the club may obtain an injunction in the courts to prevent him from doing so.

The Uniform Players' Contract prohibits the major league player from participating in a professional boxing or wrestling match, or engaging in any game or exhibition of other sports without the written consent of the

[THE CONTRACT]

club. This is to prevent him from incapacitating himself and making it impossible for him to play baseball.

If the player violates his pledge of good behavior, good citizenship and good sportsmanship, his contract may be cancelled by the club.

The contract may also be terminated by the club after requesting and obtaining waivers of the contract from all other major league clubs "if the player fails, in the opinion of the club's management, to exhibit sufficient skill or competitive ability to qualify or continue as a member of the club's team."

If it does so, the club asks waivers from the other major league teams stating that they are for the purpose of terminating the contract. However, upon receipt of the waiver request, any other major league club may claim the assignment of the player's contract at a waiver price of $1, the first club claiming being the one to get the assignment.

Within five days after he gets notice of the claim by another team, the player may cancel the contract himself if he doesn't want to transfer to the claiming team.

Who pays for the players' uniforms? Under the Uniform Players' Contract, the club must furnish each player with two complete uniforms.

This does not include shoes, however. Each player has to furnish his own shoes. Every player must make a deposit of $30 to cover his uniforms; at the end of the season he gets his deposit back if he turns the uniforms in.

What happens if a player doesn't show up for spring training? The regulations attached to the Uniform Players' Contract provide that the absentee player must "get in playing condition to the satisfaction of the club's manager at the player's own expense, before his salary shall commence."

Baseball rules prevent any major league club from signing any high school student to a professional baseball contract until he has been graduated, or, if he is not in school, until at least one day after his class has been graduated. Only college baseball players are eligible to move directly into the major leagues without previous professional baseball experience. It is required that a non-college player play for a minor league team before he can make the big jump to the majors.

I cannot count the number of times I have been asked by boys ambitious to make a start on a career in professional baseball: "Where shall I begin, on one of the major-league farm teams or with one of the independent minor-league teams?"

My answer is invariably: "Either one. Start wherever you can get a job playing baseball." The big thing is *to get started*. You can learn a great deal about "inside" baseball with a team of either classification. What you need most is the seasoning of experience, and this you get best in active day-to-day competition.

I do not think, however, that a young man should enter the baseball profession, if I may use the term, under any delusions of grandeur. We start the season with a reserve list of 40; by the date specified in the official national league rules, thirty days after the playing season begins, we have to cut that list down to 25, which means that 15 have gone either home or to minor-league teams.

[THE CONTRACT]

Some statisticians have estimated that if you include those who are in the big leagues prior to the date when that limitation becomes effective, the average span of a major-league career is less than six months.

I think this is an oversimplification. But regardless, it is true that there are only 400 major-league players in any one year, and these have been carefully culled from about four million young men in whom the ambition to play major-league baseball burns like a bright flame.

That means the average fellow's chance is about one in 10,000 to make the major leagues.

Contrary to the ideas of the average fan, playing ball is not an easy way to make a living. It is not easy to play a schedule of more than 150 games, some of them under the blazing summer sun of the mid-West.

A well-known ball player once told me: "It should not be called 'playing ball,' but 'working ball.' It is hard, nerve-racking work."

Now I don't think that many baseball players would ordinarily think of their work as drudgery. They work about seven months a year at baseball, and I daresay that there are a great many young Americans who would gladly do that for almost nothing.

But the average young man who proposes to carve a career for himself in professional baseball should prepare himself for an arduous climb against equally enthusiastic competitors.

In coming to the game, he should bring something to it. If he does not have the ability of a Ty Cobb, or the color of a Babe Ruth, or the smartness of a Christy Mathewson, let him bring along with him the determina-

[CONNIE MACK'S BASEBALL BOOK]

tion that the game will have been the better for his having played it, and if he holds fast to this determination and follows through, he is bound to find a place for himself near the top of an illustrious list of immortals who have made baseball the greatest of American games.

WHAT CAN YOU GET OUT OF BASEBALL?

I AM FAIRLY certain that every young man, before he thinks of embarking on a profession, whether it be medicine, law, business or any other calling in life, asks himself: "What am I going to get out of it?"

The young fellow who is considering making baseball his lifetime vocation and aiming for a place in the major leagues should ask himself the same question, just as I did when the time came for me to decide whether I was going to continue working in a shoe factory in Massachusetts or whether I was going to throw my future lot in with a professional baseball team in a little Connecticut town.

It's a big decision to make and you have to weigh all the factors. A great deal depends on how much you love the game itself, because in your first few years of professional baseball, the chances are that a good bit of what may be called your compensation will come from the sheer enjoyment of playing.

I remember Ty Cobb's telling me that he didn't start out to be a professional baseball player. He wanted to be a surgeon. But he didn't have enough money to go to medical school, and when he was given a chance to play baseball for a season to earn the necessary tuition money and expenses, he snapped at it.

When the season ended he was asked whether he wanted to sign up for the next season. Ty didn't know just what to do; he didn't know whether he was good enough to make the grade in baseball. He determined to make a test; to let the owners of the ball club decide just how good he was. So he put a figure on his services which he admitted later was more than he thought he was actually worth. He wanted to see, he said, whether the club owners thought he was *that* good.

"If they give in," he said to himself, "then I'm meant to be a baseball player; if they don't, I'll quit baseball and go to medical school."

As you have already surmised, they met his figure and Ty Cobb went on to become one of the greatest players of all time.

But money isn't the only reward you can get from baseball. For the top-notch baseball player, there's plenty of money, to be sure. Some players have been paid salaries approaching that of the President of the United States in their prime. In addition to their baseball salaries, they are able to add to their incomes from many varied sources, some directly and some only indirectly connected with their baseball activities.

[WHAT CAN YOU GET OUT OF BASEBALL?]

Under the rules of the major leagues, the minimum salary for a player in the big leagues is $5000 a year. You may assume, however, that there are relatively few big-leaguers working for that salary. A large majority of them get substantially more.

Baseball is more than a means of making a living. It is a national pastime. Millions and millions of men and women, boys and girls, have a deep interest in the game. They come by the millions to see it played during the course of the season. They follow it avidly. In every city, town and hamlet of the country there are baseball teams; their players pattern themselves and their style of play after the big-league players.

Radio and television, during these latter years, have brought the game directly into millions of American homes, into places where the big league teams never travel, so that the boy on the farm and in the backwoods can now familiarize himself with the appearance and manner of play of every major league star.

The four hundred select men who comprise the sixteen major league teams therefore have a responsibility as well as a privilege. Every youngster who hopes some day to be a major league star himself looks upon these players as heroes, in a sense. He bestows upon these idols a great deal of respect and admiration; they, in turn, have to live and conduct themselves in such a manner as to deserve this measure of devotion.

Oh, there are many things you get out of baseball besides money. During a major-league player's active baseball career he builds a reputation. He comes to know hundreds and hundreds of other baseball players as well as countless baseball fans. If, after his playing days are over, he decides to go into business his reputation helps him there.

Many baseball players who have retired from the diamond are now successful business men, and the chap I held up as an example earlier in this chapter, Ty Cobb, is a millionaire, having become one through his own business ability after he left organized baseball.

In baseball you get the joy of combining a profession with a game you love to play. I do not know of a single major-league player who ever wanted to do anything more than he wanted to play baseball. When baseball players or former players get together, the subject of conversation is invariably exclusively baseball.

Bear another thing in mind, also. Baseball need not be a temporary profession. It is true that the averages show most players have an active baseball life of only ten years. But if you have the necessary talent, there is no reason why you cannot stay in organized baseball in some capacity or other for the same length of time that other men engage in their chosen professions.

There is always a need for managers qualified to run teams in the minor leagues if not in the majors. Coaches are always in demand; so are good scouts. Umpires, too, are always needed, and there are literally thousands of jobs available in organized baseball for persons with administrative ability who also know something about how the game is played.

I am myself an example of the man who chose to make baseball a lifetime profession. I have been at it for two-thirds of a century or more. I owe a great deal to baseball

[WHAT CAN YOU GET OUT OF BASEBALL?]

because it has given me a great deal of happiness and a great deal of personal satisfaction. It has given me a comfortable living and a professional standing in which my sons are following in my footsteps.

But no matter what I have got in the way of material rewards, nothing can equal in value the lifetime of memories of men and events that I have received from my association with baseball:

That day in 1884 when I signed up with the Meriden, Conn., team at $90 a month as a catcher.

My debut with the Washington Senators, then in the National League, September 11, 1886, against the Phillies.

Moving to Buffalo and then to the Pittsburgh team, known in those days as the "Stogies."

My first major league managership, that of the Pittsburgh Pirates, in 1894.

Moving to Milwaukee in 1896, and my four years there under Ban Johnson—the four most interesting and educational years of my career.

The first time I saw Rube Waddell pitching for Detroit in 1898. I signed him up in 1900.

The day Waddell pitched both ends of a doubleheader against the White Sox, winning the first after 17 innings and shutting the Sox out 1-to-0 in the nightcap.

Taking over the managership of the newly-set-up Athletics in the fall of 1900.

The famous court battle over Larry Lajoie.

My first major league pennant in 1902, my second in 1905.

Jack Coombs' 24-inning victory for the Athletics over

the Red Sox on September 1, 1906, the longest American League game on record.

Eddie Collins' first day as a member of the Athletics, September 17, 1906.

Winning the World Series against the Cubs in 1910—repeating against the Giants in 1911, and again in 1913.

Taking the American League pennant in 1914.

Signing up Ty Cobb for the Athletics in 1927.

The World's Championship again in 1929 and 1930; the American League pennant in 1931.

Memories? Yes, many of them. There hasn't been a great figure in baseball in the last sixty years whom I haven't known personally. Many of the greatest moments of baseball history during the last six decades I have seen enacted; if I wasn't there for all of them, I have known the men who participated in them. Those who have forever left their fingerprints on this greatest of American games have been my friends and I have profited from the inspiration of their friendship.

I have often been asked which players I would choose if I were making up an all-time major league team; in other words, which players I consider the greatest of all time in their respective positions.

I am setting them down for you as I have seen them play over the last fifty years. They are tops in baseball:

First base: JIMMY FOXX, who was only seventeen when I signed him up on a tip from Frank Baker. Foxx was playing as a catcher for Easton, Maryland, in the Eastern Shore League. During his career in the major leagues he hit 534 home runs, second only to the record established by the great Babe Ruth.

Second base: EDDIE COLLINS, a member of the Athletics' "$100,000 infield," who saw 24 years in the major leagues as a player and established a lifetime batting average of .333. Eddie was a terrific baseball player. He never made a mistake. He was one of the greatest "team" players in the history of the game, and his superb playing set a high standard for the rest of the team.

Shortstop: HONUS WAGNER, one of the greatest names in the game. He played with the Pittsburgh Pirates and in my opinion stands without a peer at the short position. Lifetime batting average: .329.

Third base: JIMMY COLLINS of the Red Sox. He was one of the fastest men ever to step on a baseball diamond. He could hit to all fields and threw the ball like a jet-propelled rocket. I include him among the greatest baseball players I ever saw.

Right field: GEORGE HERMAN ("BABE") RUTH, whose home-run record of 60 for a single season and 714 for his lifetime in the major leagues will probably stand for many years to come. The Babe was a most dangerous man on the offensive. His bat could break up a ball game at any time and his fielding ability was not far behind the quality of his batting. Any all-time team would be incomplete without Babe Ruth.

Center field. TRISTRAM ("TRIS") SPEAKER, who in his 21 years in the major leagues earned a lifetime average of .344. In 1916 he beat out Ty Cobb for batting honors with a .386 average. Speaker definitely belongs on this all-time team.

Left field: TYRUS R. ("TY") COBB, probably the greatest ball player who ever lived. He played major-league

[WHAT CAN YOU GET OUT OF BASEBALL?]

baseball for 24 years, and for 21 consecutive years he batted better than .300. He led the American League in batting 12 times. Cobb stole 892 bases during his career, 96 of them in one year. He was daring, colorful and afraid of nothing.

Catcher: MICKEY COCHRANE, who first joined the Athletics in 1924, and is now a member of the team's coaching staff. A great catcher, an excellent hitter and a wonderful "team" player, always an inspiring "spark plug" and a leader.

Pitchers: CHRISTY MATHEWSON, ROBERT ("LEFTY") GROVE, WALTER JOHNSON, ("CHIEF") ALBERT BENDER, RUBE WADDELL and JACK COOMBS. These, I believe, are the greatest mound artists of all time. Four of them played at one time or another for the Athletics and each of the four contributed to the winning of a World Series. No list of all-time players would be complete in its pitching department, however, that did not include the Giants' immortal Christy Mathewson and the Washington Senators' Walter Johnson, whose names are now rightfully enshrined in Baseball's Hall of Fame at Cooperstown, N. Y., the birthplace of the national pastime.

APPENDIX

LET'S LOOK AT THE RECORDS

BASEBALL history is written in the records of the teams comprising the two major leagues and the thousands of players who have played on those teams.

There are also records of the minor leagues and minor league players, but the records which count for most in baseball history are those of the major leagues and major league players.

During my half-century as a major league manager, I have kept a voluminous file of baseball records covering every phase of the game. For purpose of reference, I am going to include in this book the baseball records I consider permanent and important.

[CONNIE MACK'S BASEBALL BOOK]

No book on baseball would be complete without a list of the players and others who are immortalized in the National Baseball Hall of Fame at Cooperstown, N. Y., where the great American pastime was originated in 1839:

PLAYERS

Grover C. Alexander
Adrian C. (Cap) Anson
Roger Bresnahan
Dan Brouthers
Mordecai P. (Three Finger) Brown
Morgan C. Bulkeley
Jesse C. Burkett
Alexander J. Cartwright, Jr.
Henry Chadwick
Frank L. Chance
John Chesbro
Fred C. Clarke
Tyrus R. (Ty) Cobb
Gordon S. (Mickey) Cochrane
Edward T. (Eddie) Collins
James J. Collins
Charles A. Comiskey
W. A. (Candy) Cummings
Ed Delahanty
Hugh Duffy
John J. Evers
William B. (Buck) Ewing
Frank F. Frisch
H. Louis (Lou) Gehrig
Charles L. Gehringer
Clark C. Griffith
Robert M. (Lefty) Grove
Rogers Hornsby
Carl O. Hubbell

Hugh A. Jennings
Byron B. Johnson
Walter Johnson
William H. (Wee Willie) Keeler
Michael J. (King) Kelly
Napoleon (Larry) Lajoie
Kenesaw M. Landis
Connie Mack
Christopher (Christy) Mathewson
Thomas McCarthy
Joseph J. McGinnity
John J. (Muggsy) McGraw
Charles A. (Kid) Nichols
James O'Rourke
Herbert J. Pennock
Edward S. Plank
Charlie (Old Hoss) Radbourne
Wilbert Robinson
George H. (Babe) Ruth
George H. Sisler
Albert G. Spalding
Tristram E. (Tris) Speaker
Joseph B. Tinker
Harold J. (Pie) Traynor
Edward (Rube) Waddell
John P. (Honus) Wagner
Edward A. Walsh
George Wright
Denton T. (Cy) Young

[THE RECORDS]

MANAGERS

William Carrigan
Edward Hanlon
Miller J. Huggins

Frank G. Selee
John M. Ward

UMPIRES

Thomas Connolly
William Dinneen
Robert Emslie
John Gaffney
Timothy Hurst

William Klem
(Honest) John Kelly
Thomas Lynch
Silk O'Loughlin
Jack Sheridan

MOST OUTSTANDING INDIVIDUAL ALL-TIME RECORDS

THE HISTORY of baseball has seen some phenomenal achievements by individual players. Some of them may never be surpassed. Here are some of the most outstanding:

Most home runs: BABE RUTH (1914–35) — 714
Most home runs in one season: BABE RUTH, New York (A) (1927) — 60
Most home runs in one game: LOWE, Boston (N), (1894); DELAHANTY, Phillies, (1896); LOU GEHRIG, New York (A), (1932); CHUCK KLEIN, Phillies, (1936), (10 innings), and SEEREY, Chicago (A), (1948), (11 innings) — 4 each
Most triples: SAM CRAWFORD, who played with the Cincinnati Reds from 1899 to 1902 and with the Detroit Tigers from 1903 to 1917 — 312
Most triples in one season: OWEN WILSON, Pittsburgh (1912) — 36
Most doubles: TRIS SPEAKER (1907–28) — 793
Most doubles in one season: EARL W. WEBB, Boston (A), (1931) — 67
Most singles: TY COBB (1905–28) — 3,052
Most singles in one season: LLOYD WANER, Pittsburgh (1927) — 198
Most runs scored: TY COBB — 2,244
Most runs batted in: BABE RUTH — 2,209
Most runs batted in in a single season: HACK WILSON, Chicago (N) (1930) — 190
Most runs batted in in a single game: JIM BOTTOMLEY, St. Louis Cardinals in a game against the Brooklyn Dodgers, Sept. 16, 1924 — 12
Most games played: TY COBB — 3,033
Most games played consecutively (without a miss): LOU GEHRIG, of the New York Yankees, played 2130 consecutive games, starting June 1, 1925, and ending May 2, 1939.
Most times at bat: TY COBB — 11,429
Most hits: TY COBB — 4,191
Most hits in a single season: GEORGE SISLER, St. Louis (A) (1920) — 257

[THE RECORDS]

Most consecutive hits in a single game: WILBERT ROBINSON, Baltimore (N) (1892) — 7

Most consecutive games hitting safely: JOE DiMAGGIO, New York Yankees, hit safely in every game between May 15 and July 12, 1941, for a total of — 56

Most total bases: TY COBB — 5,863

Most total bases in a single season: BABE RUTH, New York Yankees (1921) — 457

Most bases on balls: BABE RUTH — 2,056

Most bases on balls in a single season: BABE RUTH (1923) — 170

Most bases on balls in a single game: JIMMY FOXX, Boston (A) (1938) — 6

Most stolen bases: TY COBB — 892

Most stolen bases in a single season: TY COBB, Detroit (A) (1915) — 96

OUTSTANDING PITCHING PERFORMANCES

Most games pitched: EDMUND T. (CY) YOUNG, between 1890 and 1911 pitched 516 games in the National League and 390 in the American League for a total of — 906

Most games won: CY YOUNG — 511

Most complete games pitched in a single season: JACK CHESBRO, New York Yankees, (1904) — 48

Most innings pitched in a single season: ED WALSH, Chicago (A) 1908 — 464

Most games won in a single season: JACK CHESBRO, New York Yankees (1904) — 41

Most consecutive games won in a single season: RUBE MARQUARD, New York Giants (1912) — 19

Most shutout games: WALTER JOHNSON, Washington (A) (1907–27) — 113

Most shutout games pitched in a single season: GROVER C. ALEXANDER, Phillies (1916) — 16

Most strikeouts: WALTER JOHNSON, Washington (A) — 3,497

Most strikeouts in a single season: BOBBY FELLER, Cleveland (A) (1946) — 348

Most strikeouts in a nine-inning game: BOBBY FELLER, Cleveland (A) pitching against the Detroit Tigers October 2, 1938, struck out — 18

[CONNIE MACK'S BASEBALL BOOK]

WORLD SERIES RECORDS
1903-1949

YEAR	WINNER	WON	LOSER	WON
1903	Boston, A. L.	5	Pittsburgh, N. L.	3
1904	N. Y., N. L.	did not play	Boston, A. L.	
1905	N. Y., N. L.	4	Phila., A. L.	1
1906	Chicago, A. L.	4	Chicago, N. L.	2
1907	Chicago, N. L.	4	Detroit, A. L.	0
1908	Chicago, N. L.	4	Detroit, A. L.	1
1909	Pittsburgh, N. L.	4	Detroit, A. L.	3
1910	Phila., A. L.	4	Chicago, N. L.	1
1911	Phila., A. L.	4	N. Y., N. L.	2
1912	Boston, A. L.	4	N. Y., N. L.	3
1913	Phila., A. L.	4	N. Y., N. L.	1
1914	Boston, N. L.	4	Phila., A. L.	0
1915	Boston, A. L.	4	Phila., N. L.	1
1916	Boston, A. L.	4	Brooklyn, N. L.	1
1917	Chicago, A. L.	4	N. Y., N. L.	2
1918	Boston, A. L.	4	Chicago, N. L.	2
1919	Cincinnati, N. L.	5	Chicago, A. L.	3
1920	Cleveland, A. L.	5	Brooklyn, N. L.	2
1921	New York, N. L.	5	N. Y., A. L.	3
1922	N. Y., N. L.	4	N. Y., A. L.	0
1923	N. Y., A. L.	4	N. Y., N. L.	2
1924	Wash., A. L.	4	N. Y., N. L.	3
1925	Pittsburgh, N. L.	4	Washington, A. L.	3
1926	St. Louis, N. L.	4	N. Y., A. L.	3
1927	N. Y., A. L.	4	Pittsburgh, N. L.	0
1928	N. Y., A. L.	4	St. Louis, N. L.	0
1929	Phila., A. L.	4	Chicago, N. L.	1
1930	Phila., A. L.	4	St. Louis, N. L.	2
1931	St. Louis, N. L.	4	Phila., A. L.	3

[THE RECORDS]

YEAR	WINNER	WON	LOSER	WON
1932	N. Y., A. L.	4	Chicago, N. L.	0
1933	N. Y., N. L.	4	Washington, A. L.	1
1934	St. Louis, N. L.	4	Detroit, A. L.	3
1935	Detroit, A. L.	4	Chicago, N. L.	2
1936	N. Y., A. L.	4	N. Y., N. L.	2
1937	N. Y., A. L.	4	N. Y., N. L.	1
1938	N. Y., A. L.	4	Chicago, N. L.	0
1939	N. Y., A. L.	4	Cincinnati, N. L.	0
1940	Cincinnati, N. L.	4	Detroit, A. L.	3
1941	N. Y., A. L.	4	Brooklyn, N. L.	1
1942	St. Louis, N. L.	4	N. Y., A. L.	1
1943	N. Y., A. L.	4	St. Louis, N. L.	1
1944	St. Louis, N. L.	4	St. Louis, A. L.	2
1945	Detroit, A. L.	4	Chicago, N. L.	3
1946	St. Louis, N. L.	4	Boston, A. L.	3
1947	N. Y., A. L.	4	Brooklyn, N. L.	3
1948	Cleveland, A. L.	4	Boston, N. L.	2
1949	N. Y., A. L.	4	Brooklyn, N. L.	1

[CONNIE MACK'S BASEBALL BOOK]

LEADING ALL-TIME HOME-RUN HITTERS

HERE are the records of the greatest home-run hitters in the history of the major leagues:

NATIONAL LEAGUE		AMERICAN LEAGUE	
Mel Ott	511	Babe Ruth	711
Johnny Mize	316	Jimmy Foxx	534
Chuck Klein	300	Lou Gehrig	494
Rogers Hornsby	299	Joe DiMaggio	317
Fred (Cy) Williams	251	Hank Greenberg	309
Hack Wilson	244	Al Simmons	307
Wally Berger	242	Bob Johnson	288
Dolf Camilli	237	Rudy York	277
Gabby Hartnett	236	Ted Williams	265
Bill Nicholson	216	Goose Goslin	248

(*These figures are given as of the start of the 1950 season.*)

[THE RECORDS]

CHAMPION BATTERS AND THEIR AVERAGES

NATIONAL LEAGUE

YEAR	PLAYER	CLUB	AVERAGE
1900	Wagner	Pittsburgh	.380
1901	Burkett	St. Louis	.382
1902	Beaumont	Pittsburgh	.357
1903	Wagner	Pittsburgh	.355
1904	Wagner	Pittsburgh	.349
1905	Seymour	Cincinnati	.377
1906	Wagner	Pittsburgh	.339
1907	Wagner	Pittsburgh	.350
1908	Wagner	Pittsburgh	.354
1909	Wagner	Pittsburgh	.339
1910	Magee	Philadelphia	.331
1911	Wagner	Pittsburgh	.334
1912	Zimmerman	Chicago	.372
1913	Daubert	Brooklyn	.350
1914	Daubert	Brooklyn	.329
1915	Doyle	New York	.320
1916	Chase	Cincinnati	.339
1917	Roush	Cincinnati	.341
1918	Wheat	Brooklyn	.341
1919	Roush	Cincinnati	.321
1920	Hornsby	St. Louis	.370
1921	Hornsby	St. Louis	.397
1922	Hornsby	St. Louis	.401
1923	Hornsby	St. Louis	.384
1924	Hornsby	St. Louis	.424
1925	Hornsby	St. Louis	.403
1926	Hargrave	Cincinnati	.353
1927	P. Waner	Pittsburgh	.380
1928	Hornsby	Boston	.387
1929	O'Doul	Philadelphia	.398
1930	Terry	New York	.401
1931	Hafey	St. Louis	.349

[CONNIE MACK'S BASEBALL BOOK]

CHAMPION BATTERS [CONT.]

YEAR	PLAYER	CLUB	AVERAGE
1932	O'Doul	Brooklyn	.368
1933	Klein	Philadelphia	.368
1934	P. Waner	Pittsburgh	.362
1935	Vaughn	Pittsburgh	.385
1936	P. Waner	Pittsburgh	.373
1937	Medwick	St. Louis	.374
1938	Lombardi	Cincinnati	.342
1939	Mize	St. Louis	.349
1940	Garms	Pittsburgh	.355
1941	Reiser	Brooklyn	.343
1942	Lombardi	Boston	.330
1943	Musial	St. Louis	.357
1944	Walker	Brooklyn	.357
1945	Cavarretta	Chicago	.355
1946	Musial	St. Louis	.365
1947	Walker	Philadelphia	.363
1948	Musial	St. Louis	.376
1949	Robinson	Brooklyn	.342

AMERICAN LEAGUE

1900	Dungan	Kansas City	.337
1901	Lajoie	Philadelphia	.405
1902	Delahanty	Washington	.376
1903	Lajoie	Cleveland	.355
1904	Lajoie	Cleveland	.381
1905	Flick	Cleveland	.306
1906	Stone	St. Louis	.358
1907	Cobb	Detroit	.350
1908	Cobb	Detroit	.324
1909	Cobb	Detroit	.377
1910	Cobb	Detroit	.385
1911	Cobb	Detroit	.420
1912	Cobb	Detroit	.410

[THE RECORDS]

YEAR	PLAYER	CLUB	AVERAGE
1913	Cobb	Detroit	.390
1914	Cobb	Detroit	.368
1915	Cobb	Detroit	.370
1916	Speaker	Cleveland	.386
1917	Cobb	Detroit	.383
1918	Cobb	Detroit	.382
1919	Cobb	Detroit	.384
1920	Sisler	St. Louis	.407
1921	Heilmann	Detroit	.394
1922	Sisler	St. Louis	.420
1923	Heilmann	Detroit	.403
1924	Ruth	New York	.378
1925	Heilmann	Detroit	.393
1926	Manush	Detroit	.378
1927	Heilmann	Detroit	.398
1928	Goslin	Washington	.379
1929	Fonseca	Cleveland	.369
1930	Simmons	Philadelphia	.381
1931	Simmons	Philadelphia	.390
1932	Alexander	Det-Boston	.367
1933	Foxx	Philadelphia	.356
1934	Gehrig	New York	.363
1935	Myer	Washington	.349
1936	Appling	Chicago	.388
1937	Gehringer	Detroit	.371
1938	Foxx	Boston	.349
1939	DiMaggio	New York	.381
1940	DiMaggio	New York	.352
1941	Williams	Boston	.406
1942	Williams	Boston	.356
1943	Appling	Chicago	.328
1944	Boudreau	Cleveland	.327
1945	Stirnweiss	New York	.309
1946	Vernon	Washington	.353
1947	Williams	Boston	.343
1948	Williams	Boston	.369
1949	Kell	Detroit	.3429

[CONNIE MACK'S BASEBALL BOOK]

MAJOR LEAGUE NO-HIT GAMES
SINCE 1920 (Complete Nine-inning games)

DATE		PITCHER	CLUBS	SCORE
1920	July 1	Johnson	Washington-Boston A.	1–0
1922	April 30	Robertson *	Chicago-Detroit A.	2–0
1922	May 7	Barnes	New York–Philadelphia N.	6–0
1923	Sept. 4	Jones	New York–Philadelphia A.	2–0
1923	Sept. 7	Ehmke	Boston-Philadelphia A.	4–0
1924	July 17	Haines	St. Louis–Boston N.	5–0
1925	Sept. 13	Vance	Brooklyn-Philadelphia N.	10–1
1926	Aug. 21	Lyons	Chicago-Boston A.	6–0
1929	May 8	Hubbell	New York–Pittsburgh N.	11–0
1931	April 29	Ferrell	Cleveland–St. Louis A.	9–0
1931	Aug. 8	Burke	Washington-Boston A.	5–0
1934	Sept. 18	Newsom **	St. Louis–Boston A.	1–2
1934	Sept. 21	P. Dean	St. Louis–Brooklyn N.	3–0
1935	Aug. 31	Kennedy	Chicago-Cleveland A.	5–0
1937	June 1	Dietrich	Chicago–St. Louis A.	8–0
1938	June 11	Vander Meer	Cincinnati-Boston N.	3–0
1938	June 15	Vander Meer ***	Cincinnati-Boston N.	6–0
1938	Aug. 27	Pearson	New York–Cleveland A.	13–0
1940	April 16	Feller ****	Cleveland-Chicago A.	1–0
1941	Aug. 30	Warneke	St. Louis–Cincinnati N.	2–0
1940	April 30	Carleton	Brooklyn-Cincinnati N.	3–0
1944	April 27	Tobin	Boston-Brooklyn N.	2–0
1944	May 15	Shoun	Cincinnati-Boston N.	1–0
1944	June 22	Tobin	Boston-Phila. N. (5 innings)	7–0
1945	Sept. 9	Fowler	Philadelphia–St. Louis A.	1–0
1946	April 23	Head	Brooklyn-Boston N.	5–0
1947	June 18	Blackwell ***	Cincinnati-Boston N.	6–0
1947	July 10	Black	Cleveland-Philadelphia A	3–0
1947	Sept. 3	McCahan	Philadelphia–Washington A	3–0
1948	June 30	Lemon ***	Cleveland-Detroit A.	2–0
1948	Sept. 9	Barney ***	Brooklyn–New York N.	2–0

* Robertson pitched a perfect game, not a man reaching first base.   ** Newsom pitched nine hitless innings and allowed one hit in tenth.   *** Night game.   **** Opening game of season.

[THE RECORDS]

CHAMPION PITCHERS AND THEIR AVERAGES
(Based on 15 or more victories)

NATIONAL LEAGUE

YEAR	PITCHER	CLUB	AVER.
1900	McGinnity	Brooklyn	.679
1901	Chesbro	Pittsburgh	.700
1902	Chesbro	Pittsburgh	.824
1903	Leever	New York	.814
1904	McGinnity	New York	.814
1905	Leever	Pittsburgh	.800
1906	Reulbach	Chicago	.826
1907	Reulbach	Chicago	.810
1908	Reulbach	Chicago	.724
1909	Camitz	Pittsburgh	.806
	Mathewson	New York	.806
1910	Cole	Chicago	.833
1911	Marquard	New York	.774
1912	Hendrix	Pittsburgh	.727
1913	Humphries	Chicago	.800
1914	James	Boston	.788
1915	Alexander	Philadelphia	.756
1916	Hughes	Boston	.842
1917	Schupp	New York	.750
1918	Hendrix	Chicago	.741
1919	Reuther	Cincinnati	.760
1920	Grimes	Brooklyn	.676
1921	Nehf	New York	.667
1922	Donohue	Cincinnati	.667
1923	Lugue	Cincinnati	.771
1924	Yde	Pittsburgh	.842
1925	Sherdel	St. Louis	.714
1926	Kremer	Pittsburgh	.769
1927	Benton	New York	.708
1928	Benton	New York	.735
1929	Root	Chicago	.760

CHAMPION PITCHERS [CONT.]

YEAR	PITCHER	CLUB	AVER.
1930	Fitzsimmons	New York	.731
1931	Derringer	St. Louis	.692
1932	Warneke	Chicago	.786
1933	Cantwell	Boston	.667
1934	Dean	St. Louis	.811
1935	Lee	Chicago	.769
1936	Hubbell	New York	.813
1937	Hubbell	New York	.733
1938	Lee	Chicago	.710
1939	Derringer	Cincinnati	.781
1940	Fitzsimmons	Brooklyn	.889
1941	Riddle	Cincinnati	.826
1942	French	Brooklyn	.789
1943	Cooper	St. Louis	.724
1944	Wilks	St. Louis	.810
1945	Brecheen	St. Louis	.789
1946	Dickson	St. Louis	.714
1947	Jansen	New York	.808
1948	Brecheen	St. Louis	.741
1949	Spahn	Boston	.600

AMERICAN LEAGUE

YEAR	PITCHER	CLUB	AVER.
1901	Griffith	Chicago	.774
1902	Bernhard	Cleveland	.783
1903	Moore	Cleveland	.759
1904	Chesbro	New York	.774
1905	Waddell	Philadelphia	.730
1906	Plank	Philadelphia	.760
1907	Donovan	Detroit	.862
1908	Walsh	Chicago	.727
1909	Mullin	Detroit	.784
1910	Bender	Philadelphia	.821
1911	Bender	Philadelphia	.773
1912	Wood	Boston	.872

[THE RECORDS]

YEAR	PITCHER	CLUB	AVER.
1913	Johnson	Washington	.837
1914	Bender	Philadelphia	.850
1915	Ruth	Boston	.750
1916	Cicotte	Chicago	.708
1917	Russell	Chicago	.750
1918	Jones	Boston	.762
1919	Cicotte	Chicago	.806
1920	Bagby	Cleveland	.721
1921	Mays	New York	.750
1922	Bush	New York	.788
1923	Pennock	New York	.760
1924	Johnson	Washington	.767
1925	Coveleskie	Washington	.800
1926	Uhle	Cleveland	.711
1927	Hoyt	New York	.759
1928	Crowder	St. Louis	.808
1929	Grove	Philadelphia	.769
1930	Grove	Philadelphia	.848
1931	Grove	Philadelphia	.886
1932	Allen	New York	.810
1933	Grove	Philadelphia	.750
1934	Gomez	New York	.839
1935	Auker	Detroit	.720
1936	Pearson	New York	.731
1937	Allen	Cleveland	.938
1938	Ruffing	New York	.750
1939	Grove	Boston	.789
1940	Rowe	Detroit	.842
1941	Gomez	New York	.750
1942	Bonham	New York	.808
1943	Chandler	New York	.833
1944	Hughson	Boston	.783
1945	Newhouser	Detroit	.735
1946	Ferriss	Boston	.806
1947	Reynolds	New York	.704
1948	Kramer	Boston	.783
1949	Parnell	Boston	.781

[CONNIE MACK'S BASEBALL BOOK]

HOME RUN LEADERS, 1927–1949

AMERICAN LEAGUE

Year	Leader	HR
1927	Ruth, N. Y.	60
1928	Ruth, N. Y.	54
1929	Ruth, N. Y.	46
1930	Ruth, N. Y.	49
1931	Ruth, N. Y.; Gehrig, N. Y.	46
1932	Foxx, Philadelphia	58
1933	Foxx, Philadelphia	48
1934	Gehrig, N. Y.	49
1935	Foxx, Philadelphia; Greenberg, Detroit	36
1936	Gehrig, New York	49
1937	DiMaggio, New York	46
1938	Greenberg, Detroit	58
1939	Foxx, Boston	35
1940	Greenberg, Detroit	41
1941	Williams, Boston	37
1942	Williams, Boston	36
1943	York, Detroit	34
1944	Etten, New York	22
1945	Stephens, St. Louis	24
1946	Greenberg, Detroit	44
1947	Williams, Boston	32
1948	DiMaggio, New York	39
1949	Williams, Boston	43

NATIONAL LEAGUE

Year	Leader	HR
1927	Wilson, Chicago; Williams, Phila.	30
1928	Bottomley, St. Louis; Wilson, Chicago	31
1929	Klein, Philadelphia	43
1930	Wilson, Chicago	56
1931	Klein, Philadelphia	31
1932	Klein, Phila., Ott, N. Y.	38
1933	Klein, Philadelphia	28
1934	Collins, St. Louis; Ott, N. Y.	35
1935	Berger, Boston	34

[THE RECORDS]

1936	Ott, New York	33
1937	Ott, N. Y.; Medwick, St. Louis	31
1938	Ott, New York	36
1939	Mize, St. Louis	28
1940	Mize, St. Louis	43
1941	Camilli, Brooklyn	34
1942	Ott, New York	30
1943	Nicholson, Chicago	29
1944	Nicholson, Chicago	33
1945	Holmes, Boston	28
1946	Kiner, Pittsburgh	23
1947	Kiner, Pittsburgh; Mize, N. Y.	51
1948	Kiner, Pittsburgh; Mize, N. Y.	40
1949	Kiner, Pittsburgh	54

[CONNIE MACK'S BASEBALL BOOK]

HOME RUN DISTANCES
IN BASEBALL PARKS

feet from plate to fence

CITY	NAME OF PARK	RF	CF	LF
AMERICAN LEAGUE				
New York	Yankee Stadium	296	461	301
Boston	Fenway Park	302	420	315
Cleveland	Municipal Stadium	362	410	362
Detroit	Briggs Stadium	325	440	340
Chicago	Comiskey Park	352	440	352
Washington	Griffith Stadium	328	426	402
St. Louis	Sportsman's Park	310	422	351
Philadelphia	Shibe Park	331	468	334
NATIONAL LEAGUE				
New York	Polo Grounds	257	484	279
Brooklyn	Ebbets Field	297	415	343
Chicago	Wrigley Field	353	400	355
Pittsburgh	Forbes Field	300	457	335
Cincinnati	Crosley Field	342	387	328
St. Louis	Sportsman's Field	310	422	351
Boston	Braves Field	319	390	337
Philadelphia	Shibe Park	331	468	334

[THE RECORDS]

STOLEN BASES

MOST IN A SINGLE SEASON

HARRY STOVEY, Philadelphia A. A.—156 in 130 games (1888)
WILLIAM R. HAMILTON, Philadelphia N. L.—115 in 133 games (1891)
TYRUS R. COBB, Detroit A. L.—96 in 156 games (1915)
ROBERT H. BESCHER, Cincinnati N. L.—80 in 153 games (1911)

LEAGUE LEADERS

TYRUS R. COBB, Detroit A. L. (1905–26), Philadelphia A. L. (1905–28)—892.
WILLIAM R. HAMILTON, Philadelphia N. L. (1890–5); Boston N. L. (1896–1901)—797.

MOST IN ONE GAME

WILLIAM R. HAMILTON, Philadelphia N. L., August 31, 1894—7
EDWARD T. COLLINS, Philadelphia A. L., September 11, 1912—6

MOST IN ONE INNING

JOSH DEVORE, New York, N. L., 9th inning, June 20, 1912—4

[CONNIE MACK'S BASEBALL BOOK]

MOST VALUABLE PLAYER AWARDS

NATIONAL LEAGUE

YEAR	PLAYER	CLUB
1924	Dazzy Vance	Brooklyn
1925	Rogers Hornsby	St. Louis
1926	Bob O'Farrell	St. Louis
1927	Paul Waner	Pittsburgh
1928	Jim Bottomley	St. Louis
1929	Rogers Hornsby	Chicago
1930	No award	
1931	Frankie Frisch	St. Louis
1932	Chuck Klein	Philadelphia
1933	Carl Hubbell	New York
1934	Dizzy Dean	St. Louis
1935	Gabby Hartnett	Chicago
1936	Carl Hubbell	New York
1937	Joe Medwick	St. Louis
1938	Ernie Lombardi	Cincinnati
1939	Bucky Walters	Cincinnati
1940	Frank McCormick	Cincinnati
1941	Dolph Camilli	Brooklyn
1942	Mort Cooper	St. Louis
1943	Stan Musial	St. Louis
1944	Martin Marion	St. Louis
1945	Phil Carretta	Chicago
1946	Stan Musial	St. Louis
1947	Bob Elliott	Boston
1948	Stan Musial	St. Louis
1949	Jackie Robinson	Brooklyn

AMERICAN LEAGUE

1924	Walter Johnson	Washington
1925	Roger Peckinpaugh	Washington
1926	George Burns	Cleveland
1927	Lou Gehrig	New York
1928	Mickey Cochrane	Philadelphia
1929	No award	

[THE RECORDS]

YEAR	PLAYER	CLUB
1930	No award	
1931	Lefty Grove	Philadelphia
1932	Jimmy Foxx	Philadelphia
1933	Jimmy Foxx	Philadelphia
1934	Mickey Cochrane	Detroit
1935	Hank Greenberg	Detroit
1936	Lou Gehrig	New York
1937	Charley Gehringer	Detroit
1938	Jimmy Foxx	Boston
1939	Joe DiMaggio	New York
1940	Hank Greenberg	Detroit
1941	Joe DiMaggio	New York
1942	Joe Gordon	New York
1943	Spurgeon Chandler	New York
1944	Hal Newhouser	Detroit
1945	Hal Newhouser	Detroit
1946	Ted Williams	Boston
1947	Joe DiMaggio	New York
1948	Lou Boudreau	Cleveland
1949	Ted Williams	Boston

LONGEST GAMES PLAYED IN THE MAJOR LEAGUES

THE LONGEST baseball game ever played in the major leagues was the 26-inning contest between the Brooklyn Robins and the Boston Braves, played at Boston May 1, 1920. The game ended in a 1–1 tie after 3 hours, 50 minutes of play; it was called on account of darkness. Leon Cadore pitched for the Robins, as the Brooklyn team was called in those days after its manager, Wilbert Robinson; pitcher for the Braves was Joe Oeschger. Both pitchers went the full distance.

The Philadelphia Athletics figured in the two next longest games in major league records. Both went 24 innings.

In the first game, against the Boston Red Sox, at Boston, September 1, 1906, the Athletics defeated the Red Sox 4–1 after 4 hours and 47 minutes of play. Jack Coombs pitched the whole game for the Athletics and thus earned the nickname "Iron Man." Harris and Carrigan did the pitching honors for Boston.

The second 24-inning game took place between the Athletics and Detroit at Shibe Park, Philadelphia, July 21, 1945. After 4 hours and 48 minutes, the game was called on account of darkness with the score 1–1. Mueller pitched $19\frac{2}{3}$ innings for Detroit; Swift went the rest of the way for the Tigers. For the Athletics, Christopher pitched 13 innings, Berry 11.

The longest major-league game from the standpoint of time consumed was the 20-inning game between Brooklyn and the Boston Braves, July 5, 1940. The game took 5 hours 19 minutes to play and ended in a Brooklyn victory, 6–2.

Brooklyn also figured in the longest scoreless tie in major-league history. In a game against Cincinnati played at Brooklyn September 11, 1946, there had been no score by either team when the game was called because of darkness after 4 hours and 40 minutes of play.

GLOSSARY OF BASEBALL TERMS

MANY expressions used in baseball have been freely used in this book. They constitute the language of the game and a book about baseball would be incomplete without definitions of some of the words employed most often in and about the game. Obviously the list is not complete; I assume that you already know a great many of them.

Here are those I have selected:

advance   to move to the next base.
assist   credit given in the official score to fielder who assists in making put-out.
at bat   number of times player comes to batting box; not charged, however, if batter walks, sacrifices, is hit by pitched ball or is interfered with by catcher.
away   to be out, as in "two away" (two men out).
backstop   screen over stands behind home plate as protection against fouls; also applied to catcher.
back up   to reinforce player actually making play in case he misses or drops ball.
bag   any base except home. Must be 15 inches square and from 3 to 5 inches thick.
balk   illegal motion by pitcher or catcher with runner on base.
ball   pitched ball that umpire rules is outside strike zone.
base hit   fairly hit ball permitting batter to reach first base without an error by defensive team or at cost of retiring runner at next base.
base on balls   four pitched balls ruled by umpire to be outside strike zone.
battery   pitcher and catcher.
batter's box   marked-off area (right or left of home plate) in which batter must stand.
batting order   official listing of the order in which players come to bat.
bean ball   illegal pitch at or near batter's head intended to make him move away from home plate.

bench   bench in dugout to which players withdraw when not on field.
blooper   ball hit or thrown in an arc; if hit, not hit solidly; if thrown, not thrown with full strength.
box   area within which coach or player must stand.
breadbasket catch   catch of high fly with glove held slightly above waist.
bull pen   area where relief pitchers warm up.
bunt   ball that is hit but not swung at, usually employed to advance runner or to reach first base by outrunning recovery of ball by fielder.
busher or *bush leaguer*   player on small minor-league team.
cage   movable backstop used in batting practice.
catcher's balk   interference with batter by catcher, such as pushing him or tipping bat or running in front of plate to catch a pitched ball.
chance   in scoring, a reasonable opportunity to field a ball.
change of pace   slow ball or change in speed of pitch.
choke   to hold bat with shortened grip.
circuit   the four bases; a home run is sometimes called a "circuit clout."
control   ability to throw or hit a ball to the point aimed for.
count   number of balls and strikes called against batter.
cover   to protect a base against an attempt by a base runner to reach it.
crossfire   sidearm throw by pitcher that appears to travel toward home plate diagonally.
curve   thrown ball that travels on a slight curve rather than a straight line because of spin given ball as it leaves the pitcher's hand.
cut off   to intercept a thrown ball, usually to prevent a hopeless play.
dead ball   ball not in play.
delayed steal   base stolen by runner who breaks after the expected time for the break.
delivery   the act of pitching the ball.
diamond   generally the entire playing field; also the infield, which is laid out in the form of a diamond.
double-header   two games played in one afternoon or evening.
double play   a play in which two base runners are retired.

[GLOSSARY]

draft   system under which higher teams select the contracts of players on lower classification teams.

drag bunt   bunt in which ball is pushed or "dragged" past the pitcher toward the second baseman.

dugout   concrete structure in which players' bench is situated.

duster   illegal pitch deliberately thrown at batter in an effort to scare him away from the plate.

earned run   in scoring, a run scored against pitcher not caused by defensive player's error.

error   a misplay that results in a gain to the team at bat.

extra-base hit   a fairly hit ball on which the batter advances more than one base.

fadeaway   pitched ball that appears to drop and slow up.

fair ball   batted ball that stays inside the foul lines until after it has passed first or third base or has been touched by a fielder between the foul lines before it goes past first or third base.

farm   minor-league club where players are developed and seasoned.

fielder's choice   decision of fielder who fields batted ball to retire runner instead of batter, or vice versa.

fireball   fast ball.

floater   slow pitched ball with very little spin or twist.

flutterball   pitched ball that wobbles and travels slowly.

fly ball   ball batted into the air.

follow-through   completion of the throwing or batting motion.

force play   a play in which the base runner is retired by fielder's touching base whence runner has been forced.

force-out   same as *force play*

foul ball   ball that goes into foul territory after having been touched by bat.

foul tip   ball that goes direct from bat to catcher's hands and is legally caught. Batter is out only if he has two strikes against him before he tips foul.

four-bagger   home run.

full count   three balls and two strikes on batter.

fungo   ball batted to player during practice.

fungo bat   bat used for fungo-hitting, usually longer and thinner than ordinary bat.

glass arm   pitcher's arm that is easily hurt or gets sore.

good ball   ball reaching plate within strike zone; a strike.

grand slam   home run with bases full.
groove   to pitch the ball over the plate in the strike zone.
grounder   ball hit along the ground.
ground rule   special rule applying to base runners at particular ball park or field, varying under different circumstances and at different fields.
ground rule double   two-base hit as a result of ground rule.
hard ball   a baseball as differentiated from a softball.
hidden ball   trick play in which baseman keeps ball concealed in order to catch runner off base if latter believes pitcher has the ball.
hit   same as *base hit*
hit-and-run   play in which batter gives signal to base runner to start toward the next base and then attempts to hit safely the next ball pitched.
hit the dirt   to slide.
home (*home plate*)   actually the fourth base.
homer   a four-base hit; home run.
hook slide   a slide in which runner comes into base feet-first, turning body away so that only one foot will touch or hook the bag.
hop   slight upward rise of fast pitch as it nears plate.
horsehide   a baseball.
illegally batted ball   ball hit by batter one or both of whose feet are outside batter's box.
illegally caught ball   ball caught by fielder using cap or some other part of uniform to stop or catch it.
illegally delivered ball   ball pitched while pitcher is out of pitcher's box; a balk.
incurve   ball pitched by left-handed pitcher that curves toward left-handed batter, or pitched by right-handed pitcher that curves toward right-handed batter.
inshoot   same as *incurve*.
inside baseball   the strategy of baseball; planned action in a baseball game.
intentional pass   deliberately giving base on balls to a dangerous batter in order to pitch to a weaker batter following.
interference   illegal action or motion that deliberately or otherwise obstructs other team or its members in some manner.

[GLOSSARY]

knuckle ball   slow pitched ball that is held against the knuckles instead of fingertips, thus avoiding spin or twist.
lead   distance runner stands away from base; also the number of runs the winning team is ahead.
lead-off man   first batter in the official batting order; first player to bat in any inning.
league   organization of teams that schedule games against each other and abide by the same rules.
left on base   players still on bases at conclusion of the inning.
line drive   sharply hit ball that travels on a straight line instead of in an arc like a fly ball.
lineup   official list of players on team and the order in which they come to bat.
major league   American and National Leagues, as contrasted with minor leagues.
meat hand   bare or ungloved hand.
mound   slight rise in ground (varies from 8 to 15 inches) on which pitcher's plate is located.
nightcap   second game of a double-header.
no hitter   game in which pitcher allows no hits
on base   runner on either first, second, or third base
on deck   player next in batting order to the batter at the plate.
out   retirement of the batter or base runner.
outcurve   opposite of incurve; ball pitched by left-handed pitcher that curves away from left-handed batter, or pitched by right-handed pitcher that curves away from right-handed batter.
outside   away from the batter; pitch that misses side of plate away from batter.
overrun   to run past a base and risk being tagged out. It is permissible to overrun first base if no break is made for second base.
passed ball   legally pitched ball that catcher fails to hold, on which base runner advances. Charged as an error only where batter reaches first base on dropped third strike.
pennant   flag or pennant denoting league championship.
pepper game   practice before game for warming up.
pick off   unexpected throw from catcher or pitcher that catches runner off base.
pinch hitter   batter who replaces another batter in the regular batting order, usually when a hit is badly needed.

pinch runner player who substitutes as runner for another who has already reached base safely.

pitcher's box the area from which the pitcher must throw for the ball to be legally delivered.

pitchout ball deliberately thrown wide so batter cannot reach it; used generally to break up attempted hit-and-run play or steal.

pivot use of the feet in shifting position for a quick play.

pop-up a pop fly; a short high fly that can be caught without very much effort.

pull hitter batter who swings at ball too soon; in right-handed batter this results in hits toward left field; in left-handed batter, hits toward right field.

put-out the action of retiring a member of the opposing team.

relief pitcher pitcher who comes into game to replace another.

resin bag bag of resin used by pitcher to enable him to grip ball firmly.

rookie new or inexperienced player; new player in major league.

round trip home run.

run-down play in which base runner, caught between bases, is tagged out after being run down.

runs batted in in scoring, the number of runs credited as having been batted in by a player for the purposes of the record.

sack a base.

sacrifice to advance a base runner at the cost of an out. May be a bunt or a long fly enabling base runner to tag up and then advance.

sacrifice fly outfield fly deliberately hit to enable base runner to tag up and advance after ball has been caught.

scorer person who keeps the official score, usually the chief umpire.

scratch hit a batted ball that results in a safe hit although not solidly hit and therefore not fielded in time for the put-out.

screwball an incurve that curves toward left-handed batter when thrown by a left-handed pitcher.

shoestring catch catch made low, near the ground, just before ball strikes the ground.

shutout game in which one team does not score.

signals signs, actions or words by which information is communicated between manager, coaches and players.

single a fair hit good for one base for the batter.

[GLOSSARY]

sinker   a fast ball, either pitched or hit, that drops or "sinks" quickly.
southpaw   a left-hander; usually applied to pitcher.
spitball   illegal pitch in which ball breaks very sharply because pitcher has moistened ball or fingers and thus gives it extra spin.
squeeze   play in which batter attempts to bring home runner on third base by bunting safely.
squeeze play   same as *squeeze*.
steal   to advance a base without the assistance of a safe hit, sacrifice hit, put-out or error.
stolen base   base reached by a base runner by means of a steal.
strike   a pitched ball unsuccessfully struck at by the batter; a fairly delivered ball over the plate and inside the strike zone and so called by the umpire.
strike-out   three strikes against the batter.
strike zone   area over home plate and between batter's knees and armpits; a fairly delivered ball in this zone may be called a strike.
substitution   putting one player into lineup in place of another after start of game.
swing   attempt by batter to hit a pitched ball.
swinging bunt   softly hit ball that rolls like a bunt but was not intended to be a bunt.
switch hitter   batter who can bat either left-handed or right-handed with equal ease.
tag   action in which fielder touches base runner with ball. If runner is tagged off base he is out, provided fielder does not drop or juggle the ball.
tag up   to touch base after foul hit or after long fly has been hit.
take   to let a pitched ball go by intentionally.
Texas leaguer   fairly hit ball that goes over infielder's head but lands on ground before outfielder can take it on the fly.
three-bagger   a fair hit ball on which the batter advances three bases; a triple.
three-hundred batter   player whose batting average is .300 or better.
throwout   play in which batter or runner is thrown out by a fielder who tosses to a baseman, usually a force play.
toss   a light throw, usually underhand.

trap to catch a ball the moment it leaves the ground on the bounce instead of catching it on the fly.

trapped ball fly ball caught after a short bounce.

trapped runner runner run down and caught between bases.

triple same as *three-bagger*.

triple play play in which three players are retired or put out.

triple steal play in which three base runners each steal a base on the same play.

two-bagger a fair hit ball on which the batter advances two bases.

underhand a throw in which the hand is lower than the elbow, which is usually bent for the throw.

uniform the official costume, usually of flannel, which must be worn by all players in major-league games.

utility man player who is versatile and can thus be used in any one of several positions on the team.

vest-pocket catch catch of a high fly in which the glove is held close to the body at about chest level.

wait out to wait for a desirable pitch when in the batter's box.

warm-up pitch pitches allowed to be thrown by pitcher to warm up before first batter steps into batter's box.

whiff to swing at a pitch without touching the ball.

windup pitcher's motion before delivery to the plate; usually shortened or eliminated with runners on base.

winning pitcher pitcher credited in scoring with game won. Can be pitcher who starts and finishes a winning game or who comes in with his team tied or behind and completes winning game.

World Series series of games (winner must take 4 out of 7) played after conclusion of season between American and National League pennant-winners.

INDEX

Alexander, Grover, Gonzales steals home on, 10
All-Time major league team, Connie Mack's selections for, 200–203
Almeida, Rafael, 10
Almendares Cuban League, 10
American League, pennants won by A's, 199–200; pitching in, 95
Ashburn, Richie, rookie, 60
Athletics, farm club system, 22–23; hitters with, 66–67; longest American League game between Red Sox and, 199–200; minor league teams affiliated with, 21–23; players in reserve, 22; schools operated by, 23; scouts employed by, 14; tryouts, 36; 1929 World Series, 47–53

Baker, Frank, 30, 200; college ball-player, 30, 32; "Home Run" nickname won in 1911 World Series, 9
Balk, hidden ball and, 149–150; pitching rules regarding, 87
Barry, Jack, 65; college ball-player, 32
Baseball, American origin, 4
Baseball Commissioner, 189
Baseball's Hall of Fame, at Cooperstown, N. Y., 203
Baumgartner, Stan, pitcher and sports writer, 46–47

Bender, Chief Albert, 41; pitcher, 203
Berg, Moe, scholar and ball-player, 32
Bishop, Max, 1929 World Series, 48
Boley, Joe, 1929 World Series, 48
Boston Braves, World Series, 1914, 30
Boudreau, Lou, judgment used by, 125; shortstop with Indians, 124
Brissie, Lou, dependability, 167; pitcher and batter, 97; pitching courage, 43–44; war record, 43
Burns, George, 1929 World Series, 48
Bush, Joe, pitcher, 30

Cantillon, Manager Joe, 62
Carey, Max, base-stealer, 145
Castro, Jud, 9
Central America, "beisbol" popular in, 4
Chapman, Sam, All-American football, 41; Athletics, 41; tryout proves successful for, 15
Cobb, Ty, "ball hawk," 59–60; becomes professional ball player, 196; grip used by, 69; joins A's, 1927, 200; outstanding records of, 202; promises and hits homer, 62; Sam Chapman recommended by, 15; stolen bases, 144–146
Cochrane, Mickey, 48; catcher, 49–50, 102; catcher, "spark plug," coach,

[INDEX]

Cochrane (*continued*) 203; Portland club bought to secure services of, 50
Collins, Eddie, base-stealer, 28, 145; brainpower, 125; Columbia University athlete, 26–27; Columbia varsity nine, 41; debut of, 27; great team player, 202; joins A's, 1906, 200; plays under name of "Eddie Sullivan," 27; positions played by, 28
Collins, Jimmy, third base expert, 202
Coombs, Jack, college ball-player, 32; 24-inning victory for A's, 1906, 199–200; pitcher and coach, 42
Cooperstown, N. Y., birthplace of baseball, 203; Hall of Fame at, 203
Cuba, baseball in, 4
Cubs, 1929 World Series, 47–53
Cuyler, Kiki, 51

Dark, Alvin, rookie, 60
Davis, George, manager New York Giants, 8
Dean, Dizzy, cotton picker, 11; pitching star with Cardinals, 11
Dean, Paul, brilliant pitching season for Dizzy, and, 11
Dickey, Bill, catcher, 102
Dillinger, Bob, eyeglasses worn by, 71
DiMaggio, Dominic, eyeglasses worn by, 71
DiMaggio, Joe, 83, 95; slugging outfielder, 132; stride, 74–75; 1947 World Series, 139
Draft rules, 21
Dugan, Joe, third base, 120
Dykes, Jimmy, 1929 World Series, 47–49

Egypt, ball throwing and religious rites in, 3
Ehlers, Arthur H., 22
Ehmke, Howard, record in 1929 World Series, 51–53
Elliott, Bob, most valuable player in National League, 1947, 119; third base, 119
England, handball, 4
English, Woody, 51

Estalella, Roberto, utility outfielder, 10
Evers, Johnny, 30

Factoryville, Pa., home of Christy Mathewson, 6–7
Feller, Bob, speed of ball pitched by, 67; 1946 strikeout record, 158
Fewster, Chick, 146–147
Foxx, Jimmy, first base, 112; hitter, 39; home run hitter, 67; 534 home runs, 200; weight, 39; 1929 World Series, 47–49
France, tennis, 4

Gehrig, Lou, first base, 112; hitting, 113
Gionfriddo, Al, Dodgers' utility man, 139; sensational catch in 1947 World Series, made by, 139
Gonzales, Miguel (Mike), anecdotes, 10–11; catcher and coach, 10–11
Gowdy, Hank, 30
Gray, Bill, catching pad invented by, 100
Greeks, handball played by, 3
Greenberg, Hank, ability to clout, 113; first base, 112; weight, 39
Griffith, Clark, 26; as manager of the Reds, 9–10
Grimm, Charlie, 51
Grove, Robert ("Lefty"), mound artist, 203; price paid for, 50; 1929 World Series, 49
Guerra, Fermin (Mike), catcher, 10

Haas, Mule, 1929 World Series, 48
Henrich, Tommy, 1941 World Series, 101
Herman, Babe, base-running negligence, 146–147
Hidden ball, trick worked with, 149
Hitters, outstanding, with A's and opposing teams, 66–67
Homer, writes of handball, 3
Hooper, Bob, 22
Hornsby, Rogers, 51; avoidance of eyestrain, 71
Hubbell, Carl, "screwball" pitcher, 92
Huggins, Miller, Gonzales and, 10–11

i i

[INDEX]

Japanese, baseball fans, 4
Johnson, Ban, 199
Johnson, Walter, "Big Train," with Washington Senators, 63–64; Cobb homers off, 62; in Hall of Fame, 203
Joost, Eddie, A's "sparked up" by, 124; shortstop, 124

Keeler, Wee Willie, 59
Kling, Johnny, catcher, 102

Lajoie, Larry, 199
Latin-American World Series, 5
Luque, Adolfo, famed Giants' pitcher, 10
Lush, Billy, 27

McCahan, Bill, pitches no-hit, no-run game, 41–42
McCarthy, Joe, 48; manager of Yankees, 45–46
McGraw, John, 26; Gonzales and, 11; manager Baltimore Orioles, 7; manager New York Giants, 7; strategy, 7
Mack, Connie, buckskin glove used by, 99; catcher, 96; catcher with East Brookfield, Mass., team, 98; code of conduct, 34–35; early catching experiences, 98–100; outstanding events in career of, 198–200; weight, 98–99
Major-Minor Agreement, 18–22
Malone, Pat, 49
Mann, Les, 30
Marion, Marty, shortstop, 125, 128
Marsans, Armando, 10
Martin, Pepper, base-stealer, 145; Cardinals' star in 1931 World Series, 11; start of, 11
Mathewson, Christy, boyhood pitching by, 7–8; character of, 8–9; "fadeaway" delivery, 8, 92; Giants win services of, 8; in Hall of Fame, 203; nicknamed "Husk" by schoolmates, 7
Mexico, organized league in, 4
Miller, Bing, 1929 World Series, 47–49
Minor Leagues, 17–23; Athletics and, 21–23

Mize, Johnny, first base, 112
Moran, Herb, 30
Mostil, Johnny, alert White Sox outfielder, 63–64
Murphy, Danny, positions played by, 28

National Association of Professional Baseball, 18–22
Nehf, Art, pitcher, 48

Ott, Mel, home runs, 39; originally catcher, 25; professional at sixteen, 25; stride, 73; weight and height, 39
Owen, Mickey, catcher for Dodgers, 101

Pan-American countries, World Series, 5
Pitcher, distance between batter and, 67; precision required by, 84
Pitching plate, size, 86
Plank, Eddie, 41

Quito, Ecuador, baseball teams in, 5

Red Sox, longest American League game against A's, 199–200
Reiser, Pete, base-stealer, 145
Rickey, Branch, 145
Rizzuto, Phil, bunting specialist, 78–79; Dodgers reject, 16; most valuable player, American League, 1949, 124; shortstop, 124; Yankees' 1949 pennant aid, 16
Robinson, Jackie, base-stealing, 144–145; lead taken by, 150
Rommel, Eddie, pitches victory against Cleveland, 1924, 46–47; 1929 World Series, 47–49
Root, Charlie, pitcher, 47–48, 61
"Rubber," size, 86
Ruth, Babe, batting outfielder, 132; confidence, 60–61; homer hit where indicated by, 61; ignores order to bunt, 45–46; major league records, 202; pitcher, 133; strategy, 159–160; weight, 39, 61

i i i

[INDEX]

Schang, Wally, catcher, 64–65
Schreck, Ossie, catcher, 102
Scouts, Athletics employ twenty professional, 14
Shaeffer, Herman, homer by, 62–63
Shantz, Bobby, height of pitcher, 82; record with Lincoln, Neb., club, 82
Simmons, Al, "Bucket Foot," 75; 1929 World Series, 47–49
South America, pastime of baseball in, 5
Speaker, Tris, lifetime batting average, 202; outfielder, 132; technique used by, 138
Stagg, Amos Alonzo, 99
Strike zone, 84

Terry, Bill, first base, 112
Thorpe, Jim, 41
Trautman, George M., 18
Traynor, Pie, third base, 120

Uniform Players' Contract, adopted 1947, 188–191
University of Quito, sports program includes baseball, 5

Vance, Dazzy, 146–147

Waddell, Rube, 50; signing of, 1900, 199; strike-out pitcher, 158; 1904 strikeout record, 158; winning both ends of a double header against White Sox, by, 199
Wagner, Honus, immortal, 125; lifetime batting average, 202
Walsh, Ed, pitcher, 27
Waner, Paul, eyeglasses worn by, 71
Whitney, Jim, pitcher, 96
Williams, Ted, 83, 95; Brissie strikes out, 44; salary, 186; slugger, 132; wrist technique, 77
Wilson, Hack, 48
World Series, 1929, A's vs. Cubs, 47–53; A's victories, 200; Braves vs. A's, 30; Dodgers vs. Yankees, 101; Yankees vs. Cubs, 61; Yankees vs. Dodgers, 139
World War II, baseball popularized during, 4
Wyse, Hank, 22

Yankees, rally, 1941 World Series, 101
Yucatan, Mayas and ball playing, 3

A NOTE ON THE TYPE
IN WHICH THIS BOOK IS SET

This book is set in Monotype BASKERVILLE, a facsimile cutting from type cast from the original matrices of a face designed by John Baskerville. The original face was the forerunner of the "modern" group of type faces.

John Baskerville (1706–75), of Birmingham, England, a writing-master, with a special renown for cutting inscriptions in stone, began experimenting about 1750 with punch-cutting and making typographical material. It was not until 1757 that he published his first work, a Virgil in royal quarto, with great-primer letters. This was followed by his famous editions of Milton, the Bible, the Book of Common Prayer, and several Latin classic authors. His types, at first criticized as unnecessarily slender, delicate, and feminine, in time were recognized as both distinct and elegant, and his types as well as his printing were greatly admired. Four years after his death Baskerville's widow sold all his punches and matrices to the Société Littéraire-typographique, which used some of the types for the sumptuous Kehl edition of Voltaire's works in seventy volumes.

Composed, printed, and bound by Kingsport Press, Inc., Kingsport, Tennessee.